Handmade Greeting Cards

Handmade Greeting Cards

Written and Illustrated by
Maureen Crawford

 Sterling Publishing Co., Inc.   New York

Edited by Claire Wilson
Interior color photography by
Nancy Palubniak

Library of Congress Cataloging-in-Publication Data

Crawford, Maureen.
    Handmade greeting cards / Maureen Crawford.
        p.   cm.
    Includes index.
    ISBN 0-8069-8326-4
    1. Greeting cards.   I. Title.
    TT872.C73   1991
    745.594′1—dc20   90-28753
                                            CIP

10   9   8

First paperback edition published in 1992 by
Sterling Publishing Company, Inc.
387 Park Avenue South, New York, N.Y. 10016
© 1991 by Maureen Crawford
Distributed in Canada by Sterling Publishing
% Canadian Manda Group, P.O. Box 920, Station U
Toronto, Ontario, Canada M8Z 5P9
Distributed in Great Britain and Europe by Cassell PLC
Villiers House, 41/47 Strand, London WC2N 5JE, England
Distributed in Australia by Capricorn Link Ltd.
P.O. Box 665, Lane Cove, NSW 2066
Manufactured in the United States of America
All rights reserved

Sterling ISBN 0-8069-8326-4 Trade
              0-8069-8327-2 Paper

This book is dedicated with love and respect to the many creative people in my family: my parents, Bob and Joan Crawford, my husband, Dave Oudshoorn, my inspirational children, and my wonderful siblings.

Acknowledgments

I would like to acknowledge and thank the following people for their help and assistance: Barbara Bulat, Anne Crawford, Bob Crawford, Joan Crawford, Joyce Law, Dave Oudshoorn, Erika Ramirez, Marshall Shoctor, Janet Yoneda, Owen Bell and the Bell family, members of the Calligraphic Society of Edmonton, Edmonton Parks and Recreation Southwest Cultural Centre Staff, the Unitarian Church of Edmonton, and all the many students who have participated in card making workshops with me (particularly Jeanine Alexander, Colleen Howe, who gave me the kernel idea for *Aerogram with a Twist*, and C. J. Chiarizia, who initiated the idea for one variation of *Twister*).

Metric Equivalents

INCHES TO MILLIMETRES AND CENTIMETRES

MM—millimetres   *CM—centimetres*

Inches	MM	CM	Inches	CM	Inches	CM
⅛	3	0.3	9	22.9	30	76.2
¼	6	0.6	10	25.4	31	78.7
⅜	10	1.0	11	27.9	32	81.3
½	13	1.3	12	30.5	33	83.8
⅝	16	1.6	13	33.0	34	86.4
¾	19	1.9	14	35.6	35	88.9
⅞	22	2.2	15	38.1	36	91.4
1	25	2.5	16	40.6	37	94.0
1¼	32	3.2	17	43.2	38	96.5
1½	38	3.8	18	45.7	39	99.1
1¾	44	4.4	19	48.3	40	101.6
2	51	5.1	20	50.8	41	104.1
2½	64	6.4	21	53.3	42	106.7
2	76	7.6	22	55.9	43	109.2
3½	89	8.9	23	58.4	44	111.8
4	102	10.2	24	61.0	45	114.3
4½	114	11.4	25	63.5	46	116.8
5	127	12.7	26	66.0	47	119.4
6	152	15.2	27	68.6	48	121.9
7	178	17.8	28	71.1	49	124.5
8	203	20.3	29	73.7	50	127.0

Contents

Color section appears after page 64

Introduction

One of life's most underrated pleasures is the feeling of sheer delight that accompanies the discovery of a handwritten, personal letter among your junk mail and bills. That one small act of sharing and caring on the part of a friend can put a glow on the rest of your day.

The Western world is often criticized for being fast-paced, transitory, and impersonal. Many of us are caught in this web and feel unable to make a change unless we radically shift our whole lifestyle. The "art of sharing," which is what I consider making and giving personal greeting cards, is one way of standing back for a moment, slowing down, reaching out, and making direct and personal contact with family and friends. I also find that the time I take to play and have fun looking at papers, mixing and matching colors, folding and gluing cards, and thinking about who will receive each card are soothing minutes or hours that seem to suspend time and ease tension.

For many people, kindergarten was the last time they had an opportunity to really play and experiment with art supplies. The techniques in this book do not require any previous art experience or any innate ability to draw or paint. Making creative greeting cards is an accessible art form. You don't need a huge studio to house monolithic canvases, an expensive kiln, or a complex ventilation system to deal with toxic fumes. A quiet evening or sunlit afternoon spent at your kitchen table will suffice.

Unlike many art forms, the finished work will not have used hundreds of dollars worth of time or materials. You can feel free to edit out the cards that you are not satisfied with, and you can afford to share your enjoyment with friends through the process of giving freely. The recipient of your handmade card has the choice of preserving the card or disposing of it, displaying it, or tucking it away with other cherished mementos. Friendship, community, roots, personal rituals, and sharing are concepts that are inherent in the whole process of making cards.

Card making can be an intergenerational activity. For example, my two preschoolers and my mother all joined me one snowy February afternoon in a Valentine card making session. Although the cards varied widely in complexity and sophistication, we were all able to participate happily in the same activity. Card making is so special in our household that my children are always eager and willing to work on individually made "Thank-you" cards.

The cards I make may have one, two, or three folds and may interlock or have windows or doors cut into them. Some cards are laced shut or tied with ribbons. I enjoy thinking about the whole process of card making, from conceiving a design, creating it, writing in it, and sending it. I like to make sure the person receiving it has the tactile experience of manipulating the card and savoring the anticipation of a personal message inside as they go through the motions of "opening" the card.

When I teach card making workshops, I stress the importance of discovering and experimenting with different materials (origami, tissue, parchment or wrapping paper, ribbons, wires, punched holes) until an exquisite combination is found. For example, overlapping tissue paper can take on a luminous quality akin to captured sunlight or a few careful twists and folds of wrapping paper can produce a simple yet powerful design.

The design of this book follows the familiar format of a cookbook. Techniques are explained, recipes given, and variations suggested. An example of the final product of each recipe can be found in the color section beginning after page 64.

In most of the recipes, I have given exact measurements so that you can make a card according to a prescribed formula. However, I hope that the recipes will be a jumping off point for you. You may become dissatisfied with making exact replicas of the cards in this book. Feel free to experiment and change the cards you make until you come up with something that is uniquely your own. A good deal of the pleasure of making cards can be found in the feeling of contentment and satisfaction that comes with turning an idea from someone else into something you can with clear conscience call your own. It is helpful to realize that most professional artists have more works that they would not be willing to show others than works that they are delighted with. No artist works in a void by simply dreaming up a creation. Often an exterior idea or image is used as the starting point for a work of art and it is then refined and changed until the final creation truly belongs to the individual who initiated the project.

I think that my enthusiasm for card making is contingent on my love of paper. I collect all sizes and types of paper. In fact, it is my great delight in paper that has allowed friends and family to participate in the sharing process involved in card making. I have received dozens of bits of wrapping paper from friends, such as pieces of handmade washi paper found during a trip to Fiji and French notepaper made with dried flowers.

For me, card making offers the opportunity to experiment with different art techniques, to express my creativity, and to maintain personal relationships through the art of sharing. I hope that this book will give you enough ideas that you too can share in the fun of making and giving creative handmade greeting cards. However, a warning should be given before you embark on your card making adventure! Once you have begun to make beautiful, handmade cards you will have difficulty buying commercial cards. This is not because you will be unable to find great ones, or feel that it is convenient to just pick something up, but because you will insult people by giving them a commercial card when you make such lovely ones yourself.

I find that it is good policy to have a collection of cards made up and available at all times. They will come to your rescue for last minute emergencies and can also make a delightfully unique gift in small collections!

1
Basic Tools & Techniques

The most elaborate thing about making cards is your imagination, not to mention the myriad types of papers available. The actual equipment needed is relatively inexpensive and easy to find. Please take the time and effort to acquire and use the tools suggested here. The proper equipment can make a large difference in how well and how comfortably you perform your tasks.

Essential Tools

These tools are absolutely necessary to make attractive and well-designed cards.

CUTTING BOARD

There are many elaborate cutting boards on the market, some with complex grid systems. I use a plain white plastic board sold for kitchen use. I like it because it does not dull my knife blade and because cuts seal up as soon as they are made. It also *feels* nice to cut on it, and I think that is important. For card making, your cutting board should be approximately 12″ × 18″. Some other possibilities for a cutting board in-

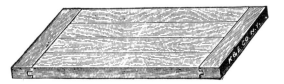

clude a piece of masonite, floor linoleum, or wood. Please steer clear of using your old kitchen cutting board. You will be unable to get it 100% clean, and you really do not want cards that have grease marks or that smell like onions or garlic.

X-ACTO KNIFE

X-acto knives can be purchased at most art, drafting, educational, or craft stores. Use one that has a #11 blade. You will save yourself a lot of grief if you buy replacement blades and are willing to *use them!!* A fresh, sharp blade makes crisp neat cuts exactly where you want them.

METAL RULER

An 18″ metal ruler with a cork backing is essential for card making. Metal, unlike wood or plastic, defies the attempts at nibbling that the X-acto blade will inevitably make. The cork

backing serves a number of purposes. First, it grips the paper and, with a little pressure from your fingers, serves to hold the ruler precisely where you want it while you make your cut or tear. Second, it elevates the ruler slightly, making it less likely for the ink from your pens to smudge or run.

GLUE STICK

A fresh glue stick is what I use for almost all pasting. The glue stick will give you a smooth, even film of glue. Glue sticks seem to have a shelf life of approximately eighteen months in my experience and new ones generally cost very little. So, don't use the glue stick you bought for your kids about three years ago, the one that is a permanent home to some wayward glitter flakes and has not always been capped immediately after use. Please buy another glue stick before you make the declaration that they are useless.

CRAFT GLUE

Most craft and hardware stores sell a white glue that will dry clear. It works well on waxy pa-

pers, on items such as origami models (which are a bit heavier than other paper pieces), and in places where the glue may show.

PENCIL

A sharp pencil is essential to make clear but erasable marks when measuring.

ERASER

A soft gum eraser works well to remove pencil marks.

SCISSORS

It is useful to have a pair of sharp, pointed scissors on hand. Some people find scissors easier to use than X-acto knives and may end up dividing cutting tasks equally between them. I tend to use my X-acto knife about 95 percent of the time and keep my scissors for the other 5 percent.

PENS

An array of different-colored, fine-tipped felt pens is useful. I make the most extensive use of pens with metallic ink, which can be purchased at most stationers and art stores. A thin-nibbed gold and silver and a thick-nibbed gold pen are essential for card making. You may choose to add other pens of varying thicknesses as well as other colors, such as copper and bronze.

BALLPOINT BURNISHING TOOL

Burnishing tools are generally used to press transfer letters onto paper. A ballpoint burnisher has a small, round sphere at the tip. These penlike items are inexpensive and can be purchased at art or drafting stores, and often at stationers. I use mine to score paper before folding it and for drypoint embossing (see Ch. 7).

COMPASS

You will need a compass that can draw perfect circles for you. It may be a high-calibre drafting tool or a part of a simple geometry set. If you can't get your hands on a compass, you may sometimes use a circle template instead.

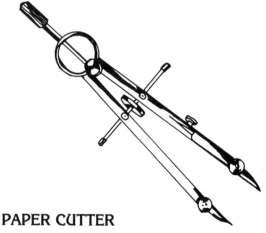

PAPER CUTTER

Paper cutters are expensive but they are very useful if you plan to shear a lot of paper or cut down large-size sheets to a smaller format. I find them most convenient for cutting large sheets, so I suggest that you buy the largest format you can afford. I don't think it's worth spending money on anything smaller than eighteen inches.

SINGLE-HOLE LEATHER PUNCH

Leather punches with interchangeable heads can be purchased at any leather goods supply store. This tool has a handle like a screwdriver and threaded heads with circle dies of various circumferences. To use one, you simply choose the appropriate-size die, screw in the appropriate head, place the paper on the corner of a cutting board, and tap out the hole with a hammer. Leather punches have the advantage over single hole paper punches in that they can go through several consecutive layers, make a hole anywhere on the paper, and can make many sizes of holes.

Useful Extras

These tools are handy, but not essential, for making cards.

COMPASS CUTTER

Art stores, drafting stores, and stationers often carry compasses that have a blade rather than a pencil on the outer edge. These are very handy for cutting exact circles.

CRAFT HOLE PUNCHES

These punches create holes of various shapes. I have ones that make stars, trees, hearts, ducks, teddy bears, and apples. I use them for both the holes they leave and the positive images they create. You can look for them in some educational supply stores or you can order them by mail from companies that make rubber stamps.

RUBBER STAMPS

Rubber stamps can be quite expensive. If you are very selective about the stamps that you buy you can get by with very few. I like some of the sea images and have purchased stamps that produce a starfish, a sand dollar, a seashell, and a fish. My collection also includes stamps that

have messages such as "Happy Birthday," "Merry Christmas," "Thank-you" and "Congratulations," in several calligraphic styles.

Helpful Hints

Before you start, here are some tips that may make your card making sessions run a bit more smoothly.

SCORING

Scoring is a method of marking paper along a fold line so that a neat crease can be made. Lightly make a pencil mark at either end of your intended fold line and then line up a metal ruler along the pencil marks. Using the ruler as a guide, take your X-acto knife or burnisher and mark the line with it. The most common methods of scoring include lightly cutting the surface of the paper with a blunt X-acto blade or with a very sharp blade and almost no pressure. Or, you can make an indentation in the paper by pressing with a blunt instrument such as a burnishing tool or the end of a nail file or crochet hook. The second method has the advantage of virtually eliminating the risk of cutting through the paper because of applying too much pressure! You will generally score the side of the paper that constitutes the exterior side of the fold. If you have a flexible ruler, a French curve template, or a very steady hand, you can also score curves.

CREATING DECKLE EDGES

Deckle edges are the rough edges found on handmade paper. If you want to get a deckle-edged look there are a number of methods you can try. Your success will be partially dependent on the quality of paper you choose. Any paper with a high rag (natural fibre) content will give you a nice edge.

One method is to fold the paper back and forth repeatedly until it virtually falls apart of its own accord. This can be a long and tiresome way of getting a deckle edge. You can also make a very firmly creased fold where you want your deckle edge to be. Then place a metal ruler along the fold line and hold it in place with one hand using a good deal of pressure. Place your other hand palm down on the paper and slowly tear along the fold line, gently pulling your paper sideways and apart. This procedure can be enhanced by first dampening the fold line with either a wet cloth or an eyedropper before you tear the paper. The most expensive method is to purchase a deckle-edged paper cutter.

EFFECTIVE GLUE STICK USAGE

When you use a glue stick, put a scrap piece of paper under the paper to which you are applying glue and run the stick off the edge of the good paper and onto the scrap. This will insure that your edges will get enough glue to stick down properly. The next time you use your scrap piece of paper make sure that you do not put the good side of your paper into an old glue spot. Cap your glue immediately after each usage! If your glue seems dry or clumpy, splurge and buy a new stick. Your old one is not worth the grief of fighting with glue clumps.

CUTTING AND BLEEDING

It can be tiresome to always have neat little borders around the sides of your cards. It is often more pleasant to have your image appear to extend past the edges of your card. In graphic terms, this process is called *bleeding*. If you are making a card where you intend to bleed your

images, apply them so that they extend past the edge of the card and trim. This will allow you to match the edges perfectly. This process is far more efficient in terms of time and effort than trying to cut to the exact size first and then attempting to match the edges.

USING PENS WITH METALLIC INK

Metallic-ink pens can be rather tricky to use. Always shake your pen very well before using it. Test how smoothly your pen is flowing on a scrap piece of paper before you use it on your card. If it seems to be jamming up, hold the pen vertically and lightly pound the tip onto a scrap piece of paper. Save the receipts when buying these pens, because some never seem to function properly and should be returned or exchanged. Other pens seem to last forever. Metallic-ink pens can bleed quite badly on some papers, so before you use your pen on your card, test it on a sample piece of paper you intend to use. When outlining in gold or silver, you should completely outline the first piece pasted onto the card, then glue the second piece in place and outline it and so on as you build your collage. If you create the whole collage first and then try to outline your papers, you may have trouble with blotting where two papers overlap. Use a metal ruler that has a small gap (due to the cork backing) between the edge of the ruler and the surface of the paper to help prevent the ink from smudging. When making several lines, it is a good idea to use a tissue to wipe off any excess ink that might have accumulated on the edge of the ruler.

If you use a thick-nibbed pen to create a border at the edge of your card, you should place a piece of scrap paper underneath and run the nib along the edge so that the line extends past the edge of the paper. This will insure that your border goes right to the edge of the paper.

2
Purchasing Paper and Supplies

A variety of paper is an essential component for having fun when making personal greeting cards. It naturally follows that finding out where to purchase paper and supplies is an important element in card making. You will probably develop a habit of collecting and cherishing expensive and exotic papers as a natural outcome of becoming a devoted, creative greeting card maker. However, such a habit is by no means necessary to make lovely cards.

One of the pleasures in making cards is being resourceful in where and how you find inexpensive and wonderful papers. This chapter will give you numerous suggestions as to where you can buy supplies and what to look for. The chapters entitled "Decorating Paper" and "Rubber Stamps and Embossing" will discuss in detail how you can turn a cheap piece of readily available paper into something really special.

One of the first things to think about when making greeting cards and buying supplies are the envelopes. My views on envelopes have shifted over time. I once thought it was necessary that the envelope match the card exactly and reveal something of its character, but I have now done an about-face. I like the element of surprise and delight that comes from opening a plain brown envelope to reveal a unique, handmade card! This is a convenient philosophy when dealing with the post office and when purchasing envelopes (brown envelopes are available in almost every size imaginable). If you are

planning to stray from the craft envelope approach, you will need to consider what you are going to do *before* you start making your cards. Getting an envelope to match your card is far harder than tailor-making a card to fit an envelope. If you intend to send the card(s) by mail, please check with the post office as to the sizes they will accept and the price they will charge for odd-sized envelopes.

Although a large collection of different papers is wonderful to have, you can easily make most of the cards in this book by carefully selecting three or four papers that complement each other. You could easily spend a whole work period making cards that are simply combinations and permutations of these. The paper basics necessary for making cards are:

(1) either commercial card blanks or lightweight card stock, which can be cut to size.
(2) one or two complementary pieces of colored plain paper, card stock, or plain origami paper.
(3) one piece of ornate paper, such as wrapping paper or chiyogami (fancy, decorated origami paper, see "Origami Additions").

Wrapping papers can be used extensively. They are readily available and come in a wide range of textures, patterns, and colors. When choosing wrapping paper, look for very fine patterns that repeat, such as tiny stars on a colored background, or ones without a pattern, such as metallic, iridescent, or blended-color papers. Steer clear of papers with figures on them, they get lost when making cards. It is very easy to get carried away with the acquisition of papers, but you really need very little to focus your attention and to create wonderful cards. Most supplies are readily available from a variety of sources to anyone who has access to an urban area. I have included some of the best here.

CALLIGRAPHIC SOCIETIES

Calligraphic societies are a gold mine! They are most likely your quickest way to find out what supplies are available locally. Often, membership will allow you to make purchases at local art supply stores and stationers at a discount. Some calligraphic societies have accounts with paper wholesalers and can buy a broader selection of paper and card stock than you would be able to purchase commercially and at far better prices. The calligraphic society that I belong to has a fourfold library that includes a wide variety of rubber stamps, books on almost everything dealing with paper, newsletters full of pointers and valuable information from other societies, and mail order catalogues for virtually anything you might ever need for making greeting cards. Other perks of membership include workshops on paper crafts, a local newsletter, the fun of meeting and talking to people with similar interests, and the natural inspiration that comes from seeing what others are doing.

Calligraphic societies can be tricky to find. They are frequently not listed in the telephone book. Your best bet is to find an adult education organization that offers calligraphy and to get in touch with the instructor. You can also check to see if individual calligraphers or scribes are listed in your local yellow pages. Another possibility is that art or stationery stores may know of local groups.

STATIONERY STORES

Stationery stores are your best source for craft envelopes. They also tend to carry items such as metallic-ink pens, X-acto knives, metal rulers, and hole punches. Some stationers may even carry an impressive range of rubber stamps, colored ink pads, and thermal embossing powders. A little time spent wandering around a stationery store will reveal a wide assortment of unusual knickknacks that can be put to good use. Large independent stationers located in commercial areas seem to carry the widest variety of supplies and are often the most open to requests for special orders. Some stationers carry blank cards and envelopes that may be purchased individually or in lots of ten, fifty, or a hundred (usually at a discount).

ART SUPPLY STORES

If you are unaware of local art stores, they can easily be found in the yellow pages. They carry paints, inks, markers, glues, and specialty papers in different weights and colors. However, they rarely carry envelopes, and their papers are generally sold in large sheets that must be cut down for card making. The staff tends to be very knowledgeable and can tell which papers are good for folding and which accept paint and glue well. If you are having a hard time finding blank cards at a reasonable price or want to use unique folds for your cards, then the perfect solution is a large piece of lightweight card stock or a heavy weight paper that you can cut down. Remember to consider envelopes before you make your first cuts!

EDUCATIONAL SUPPLY STORES

Prices are often lower at educational supply stores than they are at art supply stores. The staff's knowledge about paper will not likely be as good as at the art stores nor will the quality of the paper. However, scissors, rulers, stickers, glue sticks, lightweight card stock, ribbons, origami paper, X-acto knives, rubber stamps, and ink pads usually can be purchased cheaply in educational supply stores.

CRAFT STORES

Craft stores are good places to find glue, sequins, and origami papers. Some craft stores, particularly model stores, specialize in paper crafts of all kinds.

MAIL ORDER

If you cannot find something in your local marketplace, you can pretty well count on being able to purchase it by mail. Calligraphy guilds frequently have a collection of mail order catalogues. If you know of a good supply store that is not in your vicinity, it is worth checking to see if they will take mail orders. During Christmas season, there are often craft fairs or craft displays at malls where you will find representatives of out-of-town companies that can provide you with mail-order catalogues. One group that it is worth knowing about is

The Friends of the Origami Society of America
Room S-1, 15 West 77th Street, New York, NY 10024-5194
(212) 769-5635

Everyone interested in origami should consider joining this excellent, volunteer-based, non-profit educational arts organization. They sell a huge selection of origami books, as well as many fine papers. They do not have a minimum order. The supplies most useful for card making are extra fancy chiyogami, duo paper (different color on each side), handmade Japanese papers, oro (matte gold, this is not a foil and is wonderful for card making) argento (matte silver), and bone folders, which are great for getting really sharp creases.

If you are ordering from another country, you should familiarize yourself with custom regulations.

GREETING CARD SHOPS

You may wonder why I suggest going to greeting card shops when you will be making your own. First, they are wonderful places to browse through and get inspiration. Second, they often sell such things as stickers, wrapping paper, and metallic-ink pens. Card shops frequently have a bin of odd-sized, colored envelopes that they sell at bargain basement prices. If you do not see a bin just ask the manager what they do with leftover envelopes.

PRINTER SHOPS

Print shops will sometimes sell what they call "off-cuts" at a nominal price. Printing presses use huge sheets of paper that are cut down to the appropriate size after they have been printed on. Usually the finished size of whatever is being printed cannot be divided perfectly into the dimensions of the huge sheet and there is an extra unprinted border that ends up being cut off. The original customer who had the printing done would have paid for all the paper used on the job. Customers seldom ask for the off-cuts, and the printers are left with paper too small for the press. They usually don't want to store it, so they must often simply throw it away. You can do your part for ecology by using these off-cuts, which are usually more than big enough to make cards. Printers who do custom jobs on specialty papers are the best ones to approach. You will not have any choice in what they have, but part of the fun is discovering materials and developing a good use for them.

CULTURAL SHOPS

Cultural shops, such as ethnic craft stores often carry papers that you will not find in other shops. Look to see if they carry wrapping paper or have a craft supply section.

ART GALLERIES AND GIFT SHOPS

Locally owned, high-quality gift shops will often carry handmade paper, fancy ribbons, and specialty pens. Many art galleries, particularly public ones will have gift shops that carry unique papercraft items.

IMAGINATION MARKETS

In western Canada, there is a network of non-profit arts and recycling associations that use the name Imagination Market. Their goals are to collect and supply materials that would normally be discarded; to educate people of all ages in new, practical, creative, and joyful uses for materials; and to encourage ideas about reclaiming, recycling, and reusing.

They run stores filled with printers off-cuts, peel-off stickers, and a wide array of other delightful things that can be used in card making. It is well worth checking to see if your community has a similar organization. If you would like more information, the main office address is

The Imagination Market
10215 112 Street
Edmonton, Alberta, Canada T5K 1M7

FRIENDS AND FINDS

If you keep your eyes open, you will be amazed at what you find. One of my favorite pieces of paper came as the wrapping around some freshly cut flowers that I was given. It was a semitransparent white with a purple, marbled vein running through it. I added some gold to the marbling with a metallic pen and had a fabulous new paper to work with. Paper is everywhere in our society and, if you are sensitive to its color, weight, texture, and quality, you may find materials that are wonderful to work with in the most unlikely settings. It is worthwhile telling friends and relatives of your interests. Some of my nicest papers are gifts that people found and bought because they knew how much I would enjoy them.

Just as I added gold to the flower wrapper, all your papers do not have to be bought readymade. One of the joys of card making exists in taking a piece of very plain paper and doing something special and unique to it. See Chapters 6 and 7 for some suggestions on decorating and texturing paper.

A Word on Calligraphy

When you send handmade cards to a special person in your life, you are sending a message that goes beyond the written word. The time, care, and attention you have put into making a card will speak volumes to the lucky recipient. Because the card is a miniature work of art, you may want to consider what your written com-

munication will look like in relationship to the visual image.

There are two main choices to make when considering your written message. You may use your own handwriting or you may make it a piece of calligraphic art. Both styles are valid and each one has its pros and cons.

Many enthusiastic card makers are reluctant to try calligraphy. This reluctance should in no way be a barrier to the enjoyment of making and sending cards. When making creative greeting cards, you are sending a little bit of yourself, a unique individual. There are few things as distinctive and unique as your own handwriting. A nicely placed, neatly written note in your own handwriting will often be as appreciated as a beautiful piece of calligraphy.

There are a few tricks that noncalligraphers can use to add a distinctive touch to their written message or to incorporate a bit of calligraphy without being responsible for the penmanship. There are a wide variety of rubber stamps in various different calligraphic styles. For example, "Thank You," "Happy Birthday," "Congratulations," and "Merry Christmas" are some of the more common stamps. These look great when thermally embossed (see Chapter 7). You can also thermally emboss your own handwriting. Most ballpoint pens will leave a sticky film that you can sprinkle with thermal embossing powder if you act quickly. Various colored pens can also add interest to a card. Just remember the rule of simplicity, simplicity, simplicity.

If you are interested in trying calligraphy, there are many wonderful books on the subject and most adult education programs carry courses in calligraphy. You are most likely to be successful if you are willing to use the proper equipment in the first place.

If you are not confident in your ability to try calligraphy but you really want a calligraphic message in your card, you have the option of hiring a scribe. The best ways to find a scribe are to contact your local calligraphic society, to inquire at an art supply store, to look in the yellow pages, or to ask family and friends if they know anyone.

Many people who make their own cards like to collect quotations to add to appropriate cards. This can be a very nice finishing touch.

If you are a confident and capable scribe already, you will have developed many design techniques of your own. Unusual colors and color blending can add greatly to a card. Careful placement of an asymmetrical design will cause the viewer to focus on the calligraphy. Dry-point embossing may be used for calligraphy. You will want to consider your written addition when deciding on the original design of the card. The calligraphy should be an integral part of the design process.

3
Unique Folds

For most people, choosing a piece of card stock, cutting it into an exact rectangle, carefully folding it so that the corners meet precisely, and feeling that they are ready to start off on their card making adventure is a fairly common beginning. However, by that time, they are already a couple of steps into making the card. Perhaps without being aware of it, they have made the decision to use a symmetrical card base with a single flap opening. One of the tricks of being creative is to constantly question what you are doing and to attempt to see everything you do from a fresh perspective.

Cards are really miniature kinetic sculptures. They have an inside and an outside, a front and a back, and moving or at least opening parts. They are dynamic creations that have color, texture, shape, and depth. Cards can just as easily be asymmetrical. They may have one, several, or no flaps. The opening may be very straightforward or may involve undoing bows or tabs or lifting various flaps.

This chapter will show you some unique folds that you can use when making cards. By being observant, you will find a myriad of unique folds in the world around you that can be adapted for card making. Next time you are in a store, just look at all the ingenious packaging techniques.

Simplicity is always the key in any good design. With unique folds, you automatically add an element of interest to your card. You very often need little more than the unique fold itself to create a wonderful card. Cards with unique folds are good to make when you want to show off a particularly beautiful piece of paper or when you are looking for something that is straightforward to make and easy to repeat.

Corners and borders are the easiest portions of a card to modify when making a unique fold. Borders are generally created by making the front section of the card marginally smaller than the back section. If the outside of the card is a different color or pattern than the inside, the border will show up nicely. Corners may also be used to create interest with cards. They may be clipped (this is a type of border) or folded. See the following diagrams for ideas.

When you create a border, the edge of your paper will attract attention and therefore must be considered carefully. Some examples of edge treatments are displayed on the following page.

When working on cards that incorporate collage you may want to consider extending the collage past the traditional border of the card. This works well if you extend beyond what would be considered the top of the card because it will not interfere with displaying the card.

The following cards are unique primarily because of the way in which they are folded.

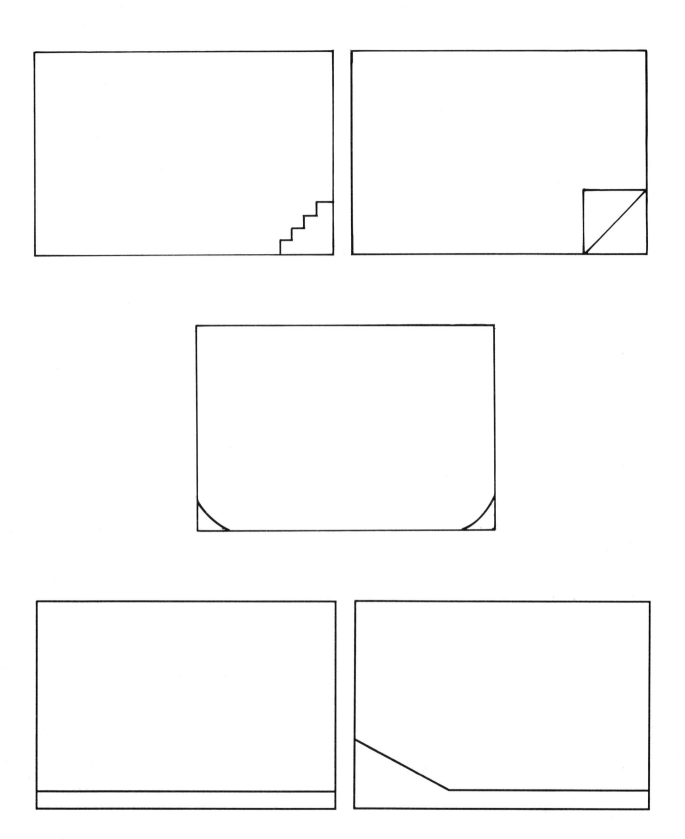

VARIOUS TYPES OF DECORATIVE CORNERS.

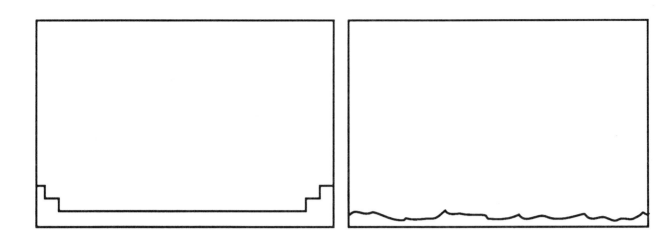

Back and Forth

MATERIALS:
- a piece of paper 4″ × 15½″ (It is difficult to make this card with heavyweight card stock, so stick to paper)

EQUIPMENT:

pencil   X-acto knife
metal ruler   cutting board

INSTRUCTIONS:

1. Cut your paper on an angle so that one side still measures 4″ and the other measures 2½″.

2. Measure 3″ from the thick end of the wedge and make a vertical crease.

3. Fold the card back and forth, accordion-style, for four folds. Make sure that the bottom and side sections all line up evenly. The easiest way to do this is to not score the paper before you fold it and to make adjustments as you crease. After your last fold, you will have approximately a half inch of paper that extends beyond the right edge of your card.

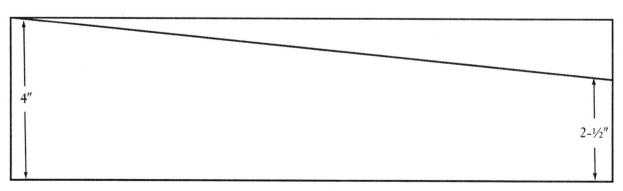

4″

2-½″

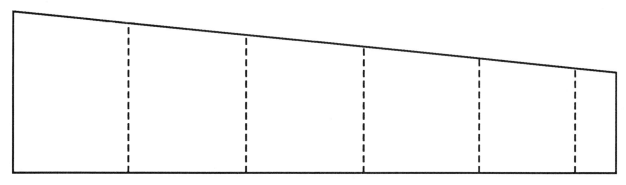

FOLD ON DOTTED LINES

4. Turn your card over and with your metal ruler and X-acto blade trim off the excess portion. This extra little tag end is useful because, depending on the weight of paper that you use, the folds will take up a certain amount of room and it is difficult to predict exactly how much this will be. With the tag end, you can trim the final edge so that it is exactly even with the side folds.

5. Add a simple sticker to one side of the card to give it a finished look.

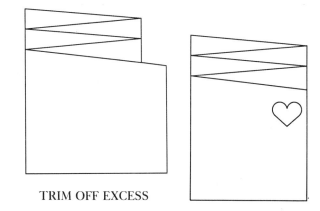

TRIM OFF EXCESS

VARIATIONS:

1. Use a felt pen to make a border along the front and back of the sloped edge of the card. You can do this as a straight line with your ruler or as a very deliberate and wavy free-hand line.

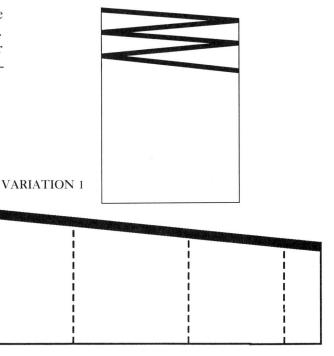

VARIATION 1

23

2. Try a "duck" variation. This card can be used easily as a birth announcement or as a birthday card for young children. Use the scissors to cut the top part of your wedge into a slanted, wavelike pattern. The more irregular your waves, the more interesting the card. Use a duck-shaped craft punch or a duck pattern to make tiny cutouts and, with a glue stick, attach the ducks to the tops of the waves.

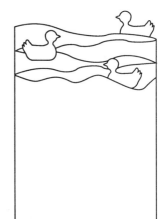

VARIATION 2

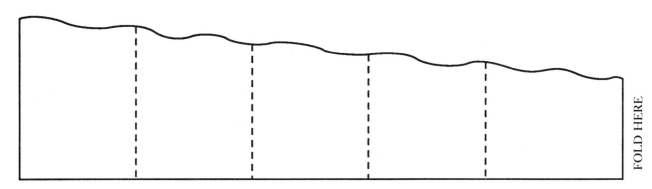

FOLD HERE

Weathergram

A friend gave me my first weathergram. Underneath the top fold was a little message that read

Japanese in origin, weathergrams are short poems written on biodegradable paper and hung outdoors to be mellowed by nature's elements. They are replaced at the equinox and solstice and become a unique way of celebrating the seasons.

MATERIALS:

- 3″ × 11″ piece of brown/beige paper
- 15″ strand of brown twine
- a seasonal poem

EQUIPMENT:

ruler   leather hole punch

pen   hammer

INSTRUCTIONS:

1. Measure 2-½" along the length of the paper and make a fold to create a flap.

2. Punch a hole in the middle of the upper portion of your flap with the leather hole punch and the hammer.

3. Thread the twine through the hole so that the recipient can hang the weathergram with it.

4. Write your poem on the remaining long section of the paper.

VARIATIONS:

1. Use seasonal-colored tissue paper strips to decorate the long portion of your weathergram and omit the poem, incorporate dry embossing (see Chapter 7) within the text of the poem, use some of the collage techniques described in the next chapter to decorate your weathergram, or simply make the fold at an angle. Weathergrams work well for quickie "Thank-you" or "Congratulations" cards and they fit easily into a standard business-size envelope.

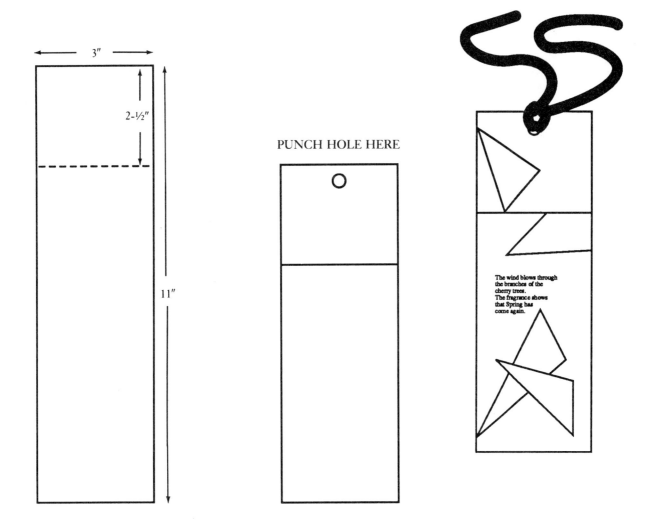

PUNCH HOLE HERE

The wind blows through
the branches of the
cherry trees.
The fragrance shows
that Spring has
come again.

Rhombus Romp

This is a very festive and easy card to make. Young children can easily participate. It's a good choice if you want to make several similar cards, such as party invitations. A rhombus is specifically a diamond shape, but any variation on the shape will work well!

MATERIALS:

- 3-½″ × 6″ medium-weight, colored card stock
- curling ribbon

EQUIPMENT:

cutting board
X-acto knife
pencil
metal ruler
leather hole punch
hammer

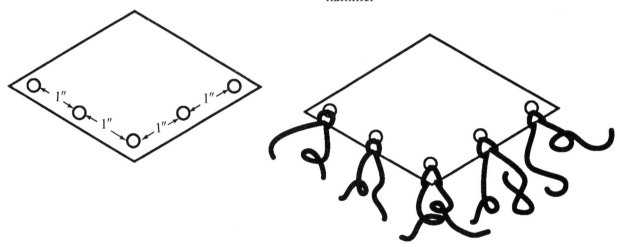

MAKE HOLES AT 1″ INTERVALS (LEFT)

ADD RIBBON AND CURL

INSTRUCTIONS:

1. Measure halfway along each side of your medium weight card stock (1-¾″ on the short side and 3″ on long side) and make a light pencil mark.

2. Use the markings from step #1 to cut your card into a rhombus shape.

3. Lay the card so that it is wider than it is tall. Make pencil marks at 1″ intervals along the lower edges.

4. Using the hammer, punch holes along the lower side at your markings.

5. Cut six lengths of curling ribbon and thread them through the holes. Then curl!

VARIATIONS:

1. Virtually any shape will work well with this, so experiment! Try punching holes all the way around the card or vary the colors and lengths of the ribbons.

Aerogram with a Twist

I got the idea for this in part from a student and in part from the old aerograms on which you wrote your letter and then folded it up to form the envelope. If you plan to send this card in the mail, it really does need an envelope, but if you are hand delivering it, the card can serve as its own envelope. A good way of sealing the flap so that it is not destroyed upon opening is to use a piece of tacky putty (sold at educational supply stores).

MATERIALS:

- 7″ × 11″ piece of paper heavier than 20 lb. bond will do. (Duplex paper, which is a different color on each side is wonderful for this!)

- thick-nibbed, gold felt pen

- 4″ square of ornate paper that complements the color of the 7″ × 11″ paper

- glue stick

EQUIPMENT:

metal ruler
X-acto knife
burnishing tool
pencil

INSTRUCTIONS:

1. Cut your paper on an angle so that one side still measures 11″ and the other side measures 9-½″.

2. Measure 6″ down both sides of the card from the straight-edged, 7-inch side and score a fold line with your burnishing tool on the exterior face. If you are using duplex paper, put the lighter-colored side facing up.

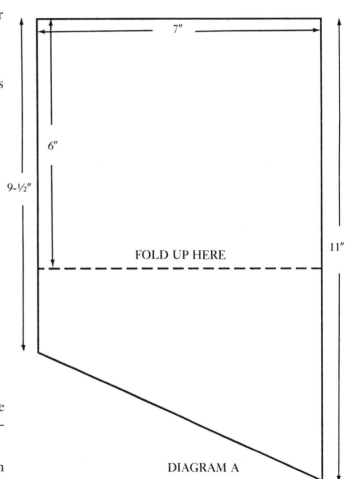

DIAGRAM A

3. Fold along the score line (see Diagram A).

4. Your paper should be about 1″ from the corner on one side and 2-½″ on the other side. Using your ruler and burnishing tool, score your paper along this angled line.

5. Fold along the score line (see Diagram B). You now have the basic fold for the card.

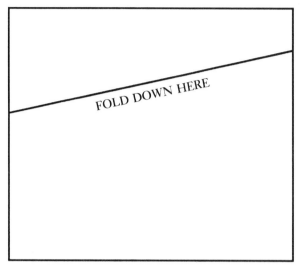

DIAGRAM B

6. Open the card out flat with the exterior side up. Then use your ruler and thick-nibbed gold pen to outline the shape of the card. Also outline your 4-inch fancy paper.

7. Refold the card and play with where you think the ornate paper looks best. When you are happy with your composition, use your glue stick to permanently fix the fancy paper in place (see Diagram C).

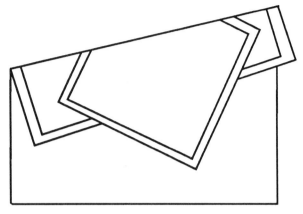

DIAGRAM C

VARIATIONS:

1. Try using a strip of wrapping paper down the whole length of the card or a large, fancy sticker in place of the ornate paper. Use a piece of your own *Meltdown* paper (see Chapter 6) for stunning results. The measurements given here can be altered slightly to vary the angle of the top or the proportions of the card. Enjoy playing until you get a card that satisfies you!

Interlocking Magic

This is a whole genre of cards that always "wow" people with its simplicity. The example given here is a card with interlocking semicircles.

MATERIALS:

- 2 strips of paper 3″ × 10″. Glue the pieces to each other back to back so that they form one strip (The easiest way to do this is to glue two larger sheets together and then cut them down

to the 3″ × 10″ format. The paper for the interior must be plain, but the exterior paper can be as fancy as you like).

EQUIPMENT:

a compass with a blade on one side
pencil
ruler
cutting board

INSTRUCTIONS:

1. Set your compass at 1-¼″.

2. With your pencil, very lightly mark the middle (1-½″) of your card.

3. Place the point of your compass at the mark and cut an arc that is just slightly bigger than ¼ circle (90 degrees). Repeat at the other end of the card (see Diagram A).

4. Refold the card and interlock the arcs as shown in Diagram B.

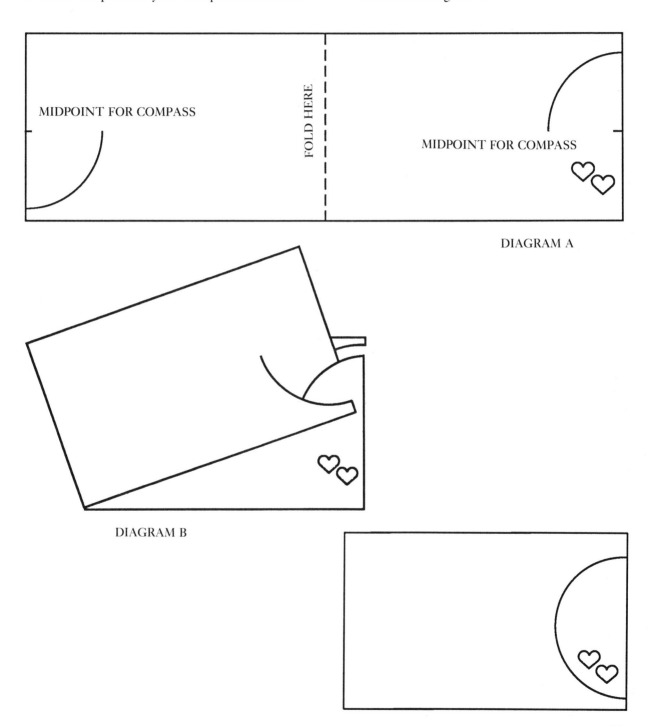

MIDPOINT FOR COMPASS

FOLD HERE

MIDPOINT FOR COMPASS

DIAGRAM A

DIAGRAM B

VARIATIONS:

1. A semicircle is not the only form that can be produced by this method. If you have interestingly shaped craft punches, such as a heart or star, you can use these to decorate your cards. You can also create a puzzle piece that has a double lock. In a small format, interlocking cards make wonderful gift tags to loop around the ribbon on a present.

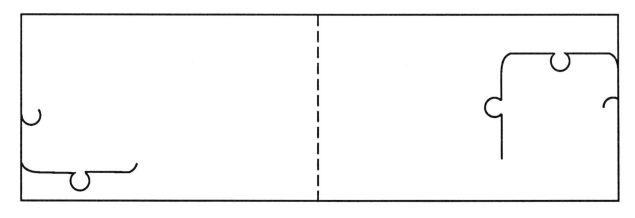

DIAGRAM A

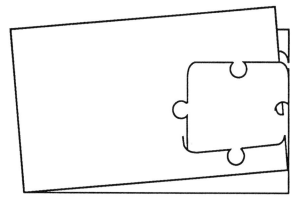

DIAGRAM FOR PUZZLE VARIATION

DIAGRAM B

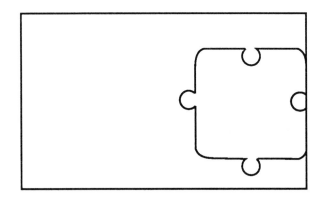

4
Collage Basics

Collages are great fun and at first glance appear to be very easy. All you need are an assortment of different materials to mix, match, and paste together. Some of the most exquisite homemade cards fall into the collage category. In order to be effective, there are a few compositional points to consider, including color scheme, material selection, composition, and simplicity. These pointers can make all the difference between creating something that you are proud of or something destined for the garbage.

Color Scheme

For most novices, color coordination is one of the major stumbling blocks in putting together a well-balanced composition. There are many books available that discuss color harmony in great detail and explain the uses of shades, hues, tones, complementary, complex, and primary colors. For those who find all this rather confusing, there is an easy way out. Use the services of a professional designer! By carefully selecting a piece of wrapping paper, wallpaper, fabric or ornate origami paper, you can utilize the color-combining savvy and skill of its cre-

ator. We are surrounded by a plethora of professionally designed items, such as magazine photographs, art books with color plates, commercial packaging, and clothing designs. There is all of nature to draw from as well. If you are constantly aware and involved in the search for pleasing and interesting color combinations you will not come up empty-handed.

Once you have found a color scheme to emulate, scrutinize it and ask yourself the following questions:

- What is the dominant color?
- What is the feeling of these colors?
- Are they soft, bright, muted, vibrant, or bold?
- How many colors are used?
- Do they use different tones of the same color, such as light blue and navy blue?

Use the dominant color as your main color, and then choose one, two, or three other colors (but no more) to use as accents. If you use two colors as accents that are not often seen in combination (such as red and pink), they can create a very unique and distinctive card. Remember to take the background color of the card into account when planning a color scheme. As you become more and more practiced at combining colors, you will gain confidence in your ability to create effective and unique color combinations of your own.

Material Selection

It is possible to spend a great deal of time on a wonderful design with striking colors and still be disappointed with the result. Look at the texture, finish, and quality of the materials before you begin. Are they rough, smooth, shiny, or dull? It is better not to mix too many of these qualities on one card. Time spent selecting materials carefully, comparing different possibilities, and standing back to scrutinize will usually be rewarded in a pleasing final product.

For collages, I most often use a blank card and envelope purchased from a stationery store. It gives the card a finished look and I can concentrate on the collage.

Composition

One of the most important things to remember when considering arrangements is that, in our western culture, we read from left to right. This is so ingrained that we naturally read art compositions from left to right despite the fact that they have no words. Assume that viewers will look at the left-hand edge of your card and then move their eyes across your composition to the right-hand edge. If your arrangement "reads" well this way it will give off a sense of balance and completeness.

Try to break the habit of thinking of the borders of your card as boundaries that you cannot cross. Cutting and bleeding your images often make a composition more interesting than if it were completely contained within a frame. Allow your paper to *bleed*, or extend, past the boundaries of the card and then decide whether you want to *cut* it back so that it is even with the edge of the card.

Complexity is the downfall of many novices. Often, people mistakenly assume that the more information and detail that they can load onto a card, the more interesting it will be. *Wrong!* Always strive for simplicity and for clean lines. The following pointers will help you achieve this:

a) Restrict the number of colors.
b) Restrict the use of patterns.
c) Have one strong focal point.
d) Limit the number of different materials.

If you follow the suggestions above you will be able to create interesting, innovative, and well-balanced compositions.

The rest of the chapter contains recipes for collage compositions. Each recipe will give you directions on how to assemble a card similar to the ones pictured on pages 33 and 35 as well as suggestions for variations.

Classic Knot

This is a very simple card, but it is one of my favorites!

MATERIALS:

- 9″ × 5-½″ card stock, folded to make a 4-½″ × 5-½″ card blank

- 3″ × 4-¼″ piece of light paper or tissue paper in a deeper shade of the card stock color. (You can also use a piece of paper made with *Soak It Up* technique described in Ch. 6)

- 2 strips of differing paper, ¾″ wide and 8-½″ long (It's great if you have handmade paper that you can tear to these dimensions. This paper is the focal point of the card so pick something that will complement the other papers nicely. These strips need to be glued to each other back to back so that they form one strip. The easiest way to do this is to glue two larger sheets together and then cut them down to the ¾″ × 8-½″ format.)

INSTRUCTIONS:

1. Glue the 3″ × 4-¼″ piece of paper to the middle of the front of the card, leaving a uniform ⅝″ border.

2. Tie a simple knot in the long strip of paper and flatten.

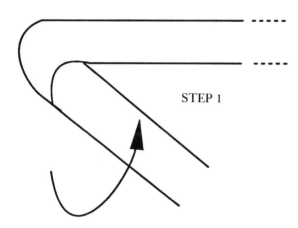

STEP 1

3. Glue the knotted strip to the card, making sure that the ends extend past the boundaries of the central piece of paper.

VARIATIONS:

1. Try placing the 3″ × 4-¼″ paper askew on the card. Experiment with the placement of the knot. Shorten the tails of the knot to form a double knot with your strip. If you cut the ends of the knot, you may want to add those pieces back into the collage.

EQUIPMENT:

pencil
metal ruler
X-acto knife
burnishing tool
glue stick

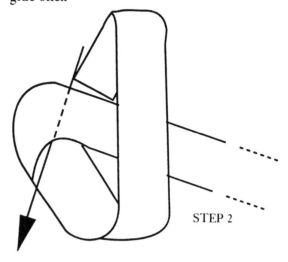

STEP 2

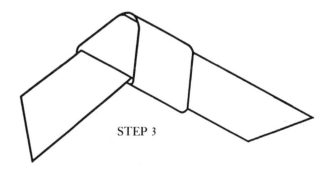

STEP 3

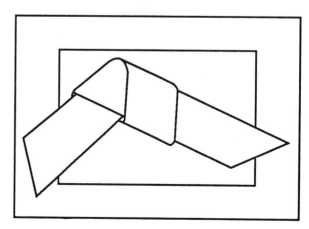

FINISHED *CLASSIC KNOT* CARD

Twister

The simplicity of this card makes it a real favorite! It is very straightforward, yet very effective. The technique consists of choosing some beautiful paper and twisting it to add interest and attract attention. The paper twists can be made in a number of different ways. One is to take two pieces of paper that go together well and glue them to each other back to back. Cut a thick strip of this double-sided paper and give it one fold. With a leather punch, make a small hole near the top of the fold and tie a ribbon through it (Diagram A).

You can also either cut a long thin strip of the double-sided paper and fold it numerous times before adding it to the card (Diagram B) or cut a long, thin strip of decorative paper that has some very strong color accents. Twist the paper a number of times, making sure that your decorative paper is always on the outside of the fold. Then choose two of your accent colors and highlight the twister by pasting pieces of those papers onto the undecorated portion of the fancy paper that show due to the folds (see Diagram C).

Remember that the basic principles for making collage cards are color scheme, material selection, composition, and simplicity. Use the twists you have just made to create your own unique collage. Some twister recipes follow to help initiate you into this technique.

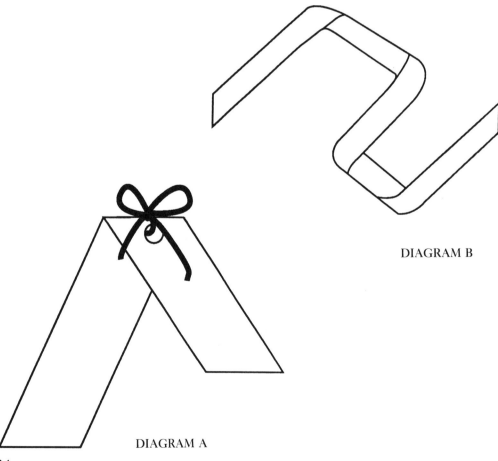

DIAGRAM B

DIAGRAM A

Once Over Twister

MATERIALS:

- 6-½″ × 9″ card stock, folded to create a 4-½″ × 6-½″ card blank

- 2 pieces of 1″ × 6″ complementary paper glued back to back

- 11″ long piece of gold cord

- 3″ square of plain paper to complement the 1″ × 6″ strips

EQUIPMENT:

glue stick
ruler

INSTRUCTIONS:

1. Fold, punch, and tie the strip of paper as indicated in the preceding description.

2. Glue the 3″ solid-colored paper onto the card blank at an angle.

3. Glue the twister into position.

Double Trouble Twister

MATERIALS:

- 6″ × 9″ card stock in a color to complement the decorative paper, folded to create a 4-½″ × 6″ card blank

- 1 piece of ⅝″ × 16″ decorative paper

- 2 solid-colored pieces of paper to match the accents in the decorative piece

EQUIPMENT:

glue stick
ruler
cutting board
X-acto knife

INSTRUCTIONS:

1. Fold the strip of paper as indicated in Diagram B of the preceding recipe.

2. Glue one color of solid paper to the upper left and lower right backsides of the decorative paper. Glue the other solid-colored paper onto the back side of the decorative paper on the middle fold.

3. Glue the twister into position.

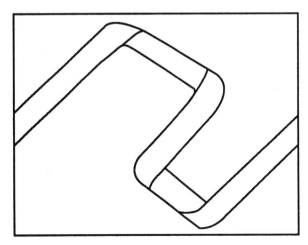

Triangles, Triangles, Triangles

Any engineer or industrial designer can tell you that triangles are the strongest shape, structurally speaking. This seems to hold true for two-dimensional compositions as well. The designs that you can come up with using triangles are endless. You can use triangles that are all identical or of different sizes and angles, or you can combine them with other shapes. When working with triangles, be aware that they tend to be viewed as "pointing" and thus have a feeling of direction or movement inherent in them. Your card should be planned with the knowledge that the composition will be "read" from left to right.

MATERIALS:

- 3 pieces of similarly colored paper triangles (The short sides should be approximately 2 to 2-½" and the long sides 4-½ to 6")

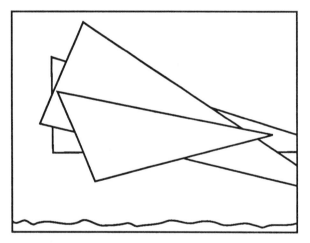

- 6" × 9" piece of heavyweight white paper
- ½" × 6-¼" piece of paper to complement the triangles

EQUIPMENT:

glue stick
cutting board
X-acto knife
metal ruler

INSTRUCTIONS:

1. Use one of the methods outlined in Chapter 1 to create a deckle edge along one of the 6" edges of the 6" × 9" piece of white paper.

2. Fold the white paper in half so that the back portion of the card is ¼" longer than the front. (You will have a card that is approximately 4-½" × 6".)

3. Glue the ½" × 6-¼" piece of paper to the inside of the card so that it creates a colored border showing through under the deckle edge. Trim so that the paper is even with the edges of the card.

4. Play with the placement of the triangles until you are satisfied with how they look, keeping in mind that they should appear to point to the right side of the card. Be sure that some of the triangles' points actually go past the edge.

5. Glue the triangles in place.

6. Turn the card over and use your metal ruler and X-acto knife to cut off any excess paper. Save the extra pieces for your next card or add them to your envelope!

Rectangles

Any simple geometric shape will give you a strong form for a collage. If you repeat the shape numerous times, it will increase the impact of your design. For example, a series of rectangles and squares cut from different papers can create a strong visual image. The composition can be used on its own or augmented with other shapes or with stickers, origami, or mizuhiki (Japanese decorative cord).

The following are two very different variations using rectangles as the primary base for the design.

Rectangles Abound

MATERIALS:

- 6″ × 9″ piece of card stock, folded to create a 4-½″ × 6″ card blank

- 2-¼″ square of fancy paper

- 2-¾″ square of bright paper that complements the fancy paper

- 2″ × 3″ rectangle that matches one of the colors in the fancy paper

EQUIPMENT:

leather hole punch
glue stick
metal ruler
X-acto knife
black, fine-tip felt pen
hammer

INSTRUCTIONS:

1. Punch a hole in the decorative paper with the leather punch and the hammer. Be sure to save the tiny circle.

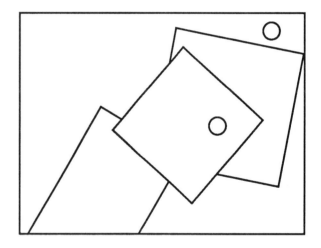

2. Arrange the rectangles as shown in the diagram, gluing down first the 2-¾″ square, then the rectangle, and finally the 2-¼″ fancy square. Trim any overlapping edges with your X-acto knife.

3. Add the circle that you punched out to the upper right hand corner.

4. Outline the rectangles and the circles in black felt pen.

Square City

MATERIALS:

- 7″ × 9″ piece of card stock, folded to make a 4-½″ × 7″ card blank
- 2-¼″ square of fancy paper
- 3″ square of bright paper that matches one of the colors in the fancy paper
- 4 pieces of 10″ ribbon or mizuhiki (2 the same color as the plain paper and 2 that match the background color of the fancy paper)

EQUIPMENT:

tape
glue stick
metal ruler
X-acto knife
clear-drying craft glue

INSTRUCTIONS:

1. Glue the plain 3″ square to the top right-hand corner of the card, leaving a ¼″ border to the top and the right-hand side.

2. Use the tape to secure the four pieces of ribbon together and tape them to the middle of the 3″ square as shown in Diagram A.

3. Glue the fancy square in the middle of the 3″ square, completely covering the taped ends of the ribbons.

4. Sweep the ribbons off to the left-hand side of the card and secure them at the edge with the help of the clear-drying craft glue.

5. Allow the glue to dry completely and cut the ribbons so that they are even with the edge of the card (Diagram B).

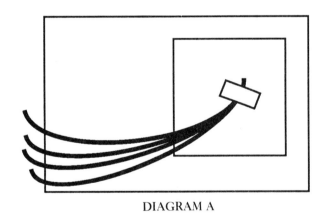

DIAGRAM A

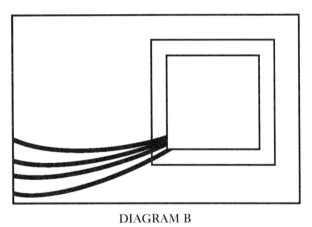

DIAGRAM B

Half & Half

This is a classical example of elegance through simplicity and balance through asymmetry. The large format of the card adds a feeling of refinement! If you have chiyogami (decorative origami paper) it is well worth using it for this recipe.

MATERIALS:

- 7-¼″ × 10-½″ piece of white card, folded to make a 5-¼″ × 7-¼″ card blank
- 2-½″ square piece of decorative paper or chiyogami

- 2″ square piece of solid-colored paper (echo an accent color in the decorative paper)
- 2″ × 5-¾″ piece of solid-colored paper (pick up the darkest color found in your decorative piece)

EQUIPMENT:

glue stick
cutting board
X-acto knife
fine-tipped gold pen
metal ruler

INSTRUCTIONS:

1. Take the 2-½″ square of fancy paper and make a parallelogram by measuring 1-½″ up from the bottom right-hand corner and cutting off a tapered piece of paper from your mark up to the top left-hand corner. Then measure 1-½″ down from the top left-hand corner and cut from your mark to the bottom right-hand corner.

2. Cut off a ¼″ strip from the right side of your parallelogram. Then cut this strip in half lengthwise and retain for the card.

3. In pencil, very lightly mark a ¾″ border around your white card.

4. Glue the 2″ × 5-¾″ piece of solid-colored paper to the inside right portion of your border.

5. Outline the border, the division between the

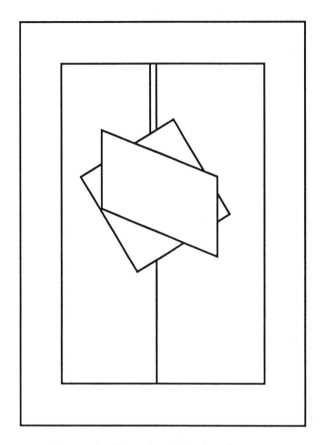

white and solid-colored blocks, and your colored piece with a gold felt pen.

6. Glue your 2″ square piece of plain paper in place according to the diagram. Outline the square in gold.

7. Glue the ⅛″ strip into position adjacent to the large solid strip and outline it in gold.

8. Glue the parallelogram in place and outline with gold.

Woven Wonders

These projects provide a marvelous way of displaying papers and of playing with colors. The weaving itself adds a subtle but lovely texture to the card. There are many, many different ways of using the basic concept of weaving to produce decorative and beautiful collage cards.

Tissue Weave

With this variation, it's best to have a large format in order to show off your weaving.

MATERIALS:

- 7-¼″ × 10-½″ piece of white card, folded to make a 5-¼″ × 7-¼″ card blank

- 3-¾″ × 5-¾″ piece of bright yellow paper

- 6 pieces of colored tissue paper, 1″ × 7″ each

INSTRUCTIONS:

1. Place the yellow sheet of paper down in front of you and loosely weave a random pattern with the strips of tissue paper, using the yellow sheet as a background. Notice how overlapping different layers will vary the opaqueness of the tissue paper!

DIAGRAM A

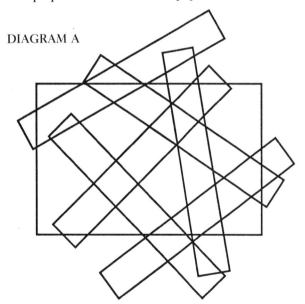

2. When you are satisfied with a pattern, use your pencil to make very faint marks on the yellow sheet so that you can duplicate your design.

3. Use your glue stick to paste all of the colored strips into position. Allow the excess tissue paper to extend past the edge of the yellow paper.

(I would suggest 2 pink, 2 mauve, and 2 sky blue)

- sheet of scrap paper

EQUIPMENT:

scissors (do not cut with an X-acto knife)

metal ruler

pencil

glue stick

4. Trim the excess tissue paper (Diagram A) with your scissors so that it is flush with the edges of the yellow paper.

5. Allowing a ¾″ border around the outside of your card, paste the woven creation in the middle of your card blank (Diagram B).

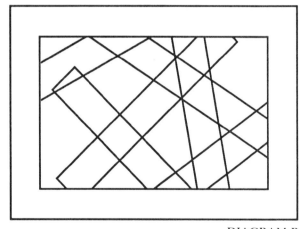

DIAGRAM B

VARIATIONS:

1. You can easily apply the woven tissue design directly onto a brightly colored card blank. You can experiment with different color combinations or apply the yellow woven portion to the card in an asymmetrical fashion. If you use a large sheet of yellow paper, you can crop the paper to the size you require and use the trimmings to form a new card.

Interwoven

What I like about this card is its purity. All you need is the card stock and the paper. This design is very three-dimensional in nature. You first view the front cover, then, as you are in the process of opening it, you see a little of both sides. Finally, you view it from the interior perspective. Remember to take both sides into consideration when planning!

MATERIALS:

- 7-¼″ × 10-½″ piece of white card, folded to make a 5-¼″ × 7-¼″ card blank

- pieces of blue, purple, and pink paper, large enough to cut into several 7-¼″-long strips

EQUIPMENT:

X-acto knife   pencil
cutting board   glue stick
metal ruler

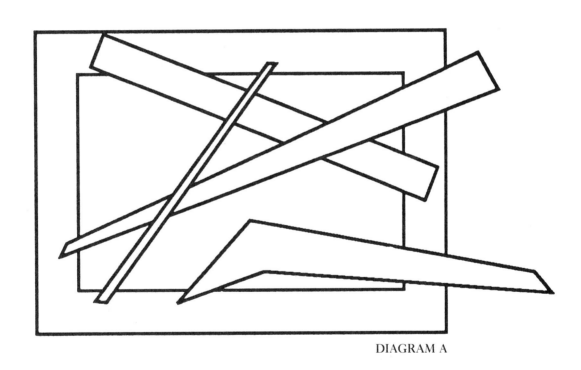

DIAGRAM A

INSTRUCTIONS:

1. With your pencil, faintly draw a ¾″ border around the edge of the card blank.

2. Cut out colored strips of paper in shapes similar to those in the diagram below.

3. Place the colored strips in an interesting arrangement on the card (Diagram A). Play with your design until you are content with the placement of all your paper pieces.

4. Make sure that your card blank is open fully and placed on top of your cutting board. Use your X-acto knife to make tiny pinpricks on either side of the colored paper where it passes over your pencil border.

5. Make a slit on the pencil line between your two pinpricks. This is where your colored paper will tuck through to the backside of your card.

6. With your papers in place, decide on a few more places where it would be interesting to create a woven effect. Repeat the same procedure of using your X-acto knife to mark where the cuts will be made.

7. Make your new cuts and weave the paper (Diagram B). Look at the inside of the card and consider its design. Make any necessary adjustments.

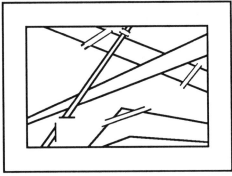

DIAGRAM C

8. Remove all your colored papers and very carefully erase your pencil border. Then re-insert your colored pieces (Diagram C). Trim any excess.

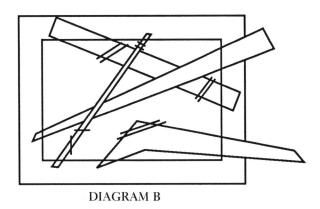

DIAGRAM B

VARIATIONS:

1. You can vary this card by using almost any kind of paper (as long as it is not extremely flimsy) or by altering the shapes, sizes, colors, and quantity of the decorative strips.

Loose Weave

This pattern is made with the classic over and under weaving technique.

MATERIALS:

- 5-1/2" × 8-1/2" piece of card, folded to create a 4-1/4" × 5-1/2" card blank

- 2 pieces of plain paper 1/2" × 7"

- 4 strips of 1/2" × 7" patterned decorative paper (either wrapping paper or patterned origami paper will work)

- 4 strips of 1/2" × 7" of a different pattern of decorative paper

- masking tape

- sheet of scrap paper

EQUIPMENT:

cutting board
X-acto knife
pencil
glue stick
metal ruler

INSTRUCTIONS:

1. Place a 6″ piece of masking tape on your work surface with the sticky side up.

2. Tack five of the pieces of paper onto the tape to form a fringe.

3. Use the other strips of paper to weave over and under the fringe pieces (Diagram A). Allow your weaving to be quite loose and open. When you feel content with your weaving, slip the card blank underneath and decide on the final arrangement. You may want to trim some of the ends so that they do not extend past the edge of the card or so that they are angled at the end.

4. Use a piece of tape along the outside right edge to hold the finished weaving together.

5. Turn the whole weaving over and with a piece of scrap paper underneath apply glue to the back side of your weaving.

DIAGRAM A

43

6. Remove the scrap paper and lay your card face down on top of the woven work. Firmly press down on the paper.

7. Turn your card over and trim the edges (Diagram B, next page).

VARIATIONS:

1. One of my favorite variations for this card is to cut out a large heart shape and make several slashes in the middle. You can then weave pieces of paper through the middle of the heart.

DIAGRAM B

Craft Punches

Some stationery stores carry craft punches that cut out specific forms, such as stars, teddy bears, apples, trees, ducks, cows, hearts, and butterflies. They are easy to use, a favorite with children, and are very decorative. As an added plus, most are inexpensive.

Hole Punchy

This is one example of how a craft punch can be used to make a very attractive card. It incorporates the compositional techniques of simplicity and asymmetry.

MATERIALS:

- 5″ × 7″ piece of midnight blue-colored card stock

- 4″ × 5″ piece of white, high-quality paper

- 9″ length of gold cord

- jar of gold acrylic poster paint

EQUIPMENT:

star craft punch   metal ruler
jar lid   pencil
sponge

INSTRUCTIONS:

1. Use the *Stardust* technique from page 68 to decorate both the blue and the white piece of paper.

2. Place the white paper on top of the blue, leaving a ½″ border along the top and the sides.

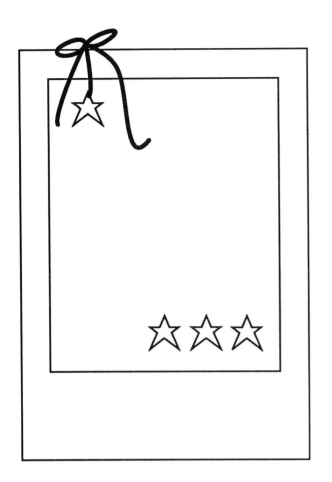

3. Punch a star hole through the upper left corner of the white paper so that it makes a hole in the blue paper underneath, as well.

4. Remove the white paper and punch one star hole at the bottom center and two more to the right of the middle star.

5. Place the white paper back on the midnight blue card and line up the upper left hand star holes. Use the gold cord to tie the two pieces together with a bow.

VARIATIONS:

1. This card can be made with any form of craft punch. Punches may also be used in making borders. You can make instant stickers by cutting paper with a gummed back. Punches can also be used to make stencils for drypoint embossing (see page 75).

5
Origami Additions

I became interested in making original greeting cards through a love of origami. I enjoyed the brightly colored papers and the incredible variety of possible models that could be produced from a single square of paper. As I attempted new and different folds, I wondered what to do with the pieces that I had already made. Many of the models were flat and suitable for decorations on greeting cards. Some were even used to create pop-up cards! These designs worked well and were much enjoyed by the people who received them. As I have continued to fold origami, the designs have become more and more complex and less adaptable to cards. However, I still find it exciting and rewarding to search for flat models that are appropriate for card making. I always try to keep things simple. Variety and interest in making origami cards come from the choice of papers and the collage techniques that I use.

I have chosen to present three very different origami folds in this chapter and to concentrate on the ways that origami models can be used on cards. Many origami books give an extensive catalogue of different models. Origami/collage cards are still the type I make most frequently and are among the most stunning cards that I have produced.

Origami originated in Japan. Traditional origami begins with just a square piece of paper, and no cuts are allowed when making the designs. Many modifications can be made to these strict guidelines (some of which I have included later in this chapter). Since 1980, there has been an incredible worldwide increase in interest in origami. Some of the most exciting modern folders and designers are British, American, and Italian.

Because of the Japanese roots of origami, I try to give most of my cards an Asian flavor. I do this by following some simple guidelines.

1. *Make the cards asymmetrical.* I tend not to line everything up, have even borders, or center the models. I keep in mind that a composition is generally read from left to right in our culture, and so I attempt to balance the card with the use of color and focal points rather than symmetry.

2. *Use an odd number.* I usually use one model, but if I am going to use more than one, it will likely be an odd number. The same is true for collage components. For example, I may use three paper triangles behind a kimono.

3. *Use Japanese decorative paper* (*chiyogami*). These papers usually have a very Asian pattern and color scheme on them. I like to show the papers off, so I rarely fold my models out of chiyogami. Instead, I prefer to use it as a background or accenting paper.

4. *Use Asian color schemes.* You can copy the color scheme used for Japanese dolls, wrapping

paper, or chiyogami. I look for a color mixture that would be considered unusual in non-Asian societies. For example, many Japanese dolls combine orange, red, and a light blue or soft purple.

5. *Use Asian-style models.* If the folded pattern you choose is an Asian image, you will inevitably have an Asian-looking card. It naturally follows that if you choose a kimono as your model, you are likely to have a card with a Japanese feel to it.

6. *Keep your composition simple.* Make sure the origami model is shown off to greatest advantage by not having other elements of the composition competing for attention. The origami figure should be the focal point of the card.

Origami models are beautiful and the pieces presented in this book are not difficult. There are, however, a number of technical points that will help you to avoid frustration if you are a beginner. When making your model, try to be very precise about folding corners so that they meet evenly and have firm, crisp creases. The more exacting you are in your folding, the more pleased you are likely to be with the outcome. As a general rule, the first time you fold a model, you concentrate on understanding the concept of how the folds are organized and how they progress to give you the finished form. Do not use your best paper to learn a new fold. It is exceptionally rare to be pleased with the finished look of a first attempt! Execute a number of dry runs before you judge yourself capable of folding that particular model to your own satisfaction.

The quality and size of the paper will influence the final product. When I am making a figure for the first time, I will often work at one and a half to two times the suggested size. This allows me to clearly see what I am doing without being concerned with tiny little creases. However, working any larger than this can be awkward and ungainly.

The choice of paper is also important. There are many different types of origami paper. The three varieties most commonly found outside of Japan are: kami, chiyogami, and momi.

Plain, solid-colored origami paper is known as kami. It is colored on the top and white on the underside. Instructional diagrams are shaded to represent the colored side and white underside. Kami comes in perfect squares, is relatively inexpensive, and accepts a crease very well. I like the crispness, the clean lines, and the simplicity of models that are made out of kami. If a decorative element is needed on the origami figure I often add it with a gold felt pen.

Chiyogami is the name given to patterned origami paper. It comes in many different designs, color combinations, and qualities of paper. I generally buy the top-grade chiyogami paper, which has intricate patterns and either gold or silver accents. This paper, with its rich colors and designs, is expensive but only a little is needed on each card so that I feel the expense is justified. Wrapping paper that is decorative on one side and plain on the other can serve as a substitute for chiyogami paper.

Momi is a Japanese paper with a crushed and crumbled look. It is a wonderful material to use because it gives your design a deep, rich texture without having it look too busy. Remember, simplicity is the key in these cards!

When folding origami models, do not use construction paper or typing paper. These papers are the same on both sides, which can make it difficult to follow diagrams, and they tend to be bulky and tear after the first two or three folds.

The origami models shown in this chapter will serve as an appetizer to anyone really interested in the art form. There are a wealth of origami books on the market today and many have simple, flat folds appropriate for card making. If you intend to buy origami books for use in making cards, make sure that you examine them for a few factors. For example:

- Do the diagrams clearly show a colored side and a white side?
- Are the models shown flat and suitable for cards?
- Is there a symbol legend in the book?

When making a card that will display an origami figure, the careful selection of materials is essential to the success of the card. I spend more time deliberating over colors, textures, and patterns than I do in either figuring out the composition or executing the design. Enjoy playing with the different paper combinations—this should be fun rather than stressful!

When a decorative paper is used in either the background or in a model, it sets the color scheme. All colors on the card should also be contained within the patterned piece. The tone of the color should be taken into consideration as well. For example, if you have a decorative piece with a deep emerald green in it you would generally try to match the same shade instead of using a pale green. If your decorative paper has gray, pink, blue, mauve, and silver you might use it with a gray card, a pink origami figure, and finish off with some silver highlights from a felt pen.

FANtasy

This is an easily made design that has many wonderful variations. I find this one has a masculine feel to it and I often use it as a birthday card for men.

MATERIALS:

- 9″ × 6″ blank in a bold color, folded to create a 4-½″ × 6″ card
- 4-¼″ × 5″ piece of patterned wrapping paper or chiyogami that has gold in it and also picks up the color of the card stock
- 2 pieces of solid-colored paper (preferably gold) that complement the patterned paper (One piece should be 6″ square and the other 1-½″ × 4″)
- narrow piece of curling ribbon the same color as the card stock

EQUIPMENT:

gold pen
leather punch with a small-size die
glue stick
metal ruler
X-acto knife
clear-drying craft glue
hammer

INSTRUCTIONS:

1. Flatten the card and glue the solid piece of paper onto the card as indicated in the diagram.

2. Glue the decorative wrapping paper into position.

3. Turn the card over and use your metal ruler and X-acto knife to cut off any paper overhanging the edge. Save the pieces you cut off for your next card or envelope.

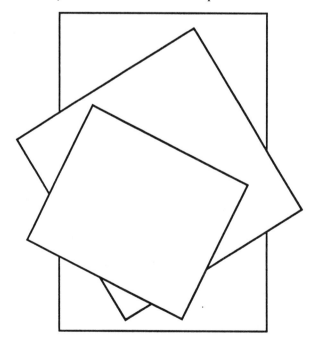

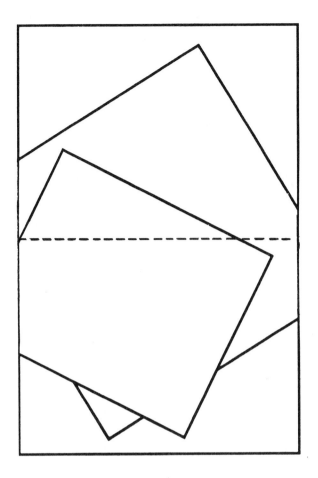

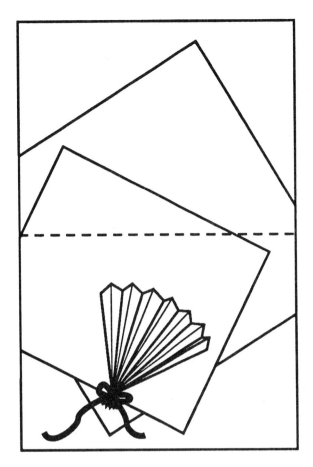

4. Outline the decorative paper with the gold felt pen.

5. Take the 4″ strip of paper and fold it back and forth accordion style to create a fan (see illustration). The creases should be approximately ¼″ deep.

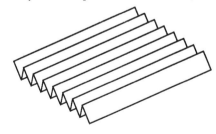

6. Take the leather punch and hammer and make a hole at one end of the fan that goes through all the creases.

7. Thread the curling ribbon through the hole and secure it with a bow. Curl the ribbon ends with the blade of your scissors.

8. Open the top portion of the fan and secure the whole fan to the card with an ample amount of clear-drying craft glue. Allow it time to dry.

9. Use the clear glue to tack the ribbon ends into place.

Dark FANtasy

This is a large-format card and it carries with it a high impact.

MATERIALS:

- 14″ × 9″ blank in a strong, deep color to complement your chiyogami choice, folded to create a 7″ × 9″ card
- 4″ square piece of patterned wrapping paper or chiyogami that has gold in it
- 5″ square piece of solid, dark-colored paper that complements the chiyogami paper
- a narrow piece of gold curling ribbon
- 2″ × 4″ strip of paper the same color as the card stock

EQUIPMENT:

gold pen
leather hole punch with a small hole size
hammer
glue stick
metal ruler
X-acto knife
clear-drying craft glue

INSTRUCTIONS:

1. Glue the 5″ square solid piece of paper onto the card, creating a ⅝″ border in the upper-right-hand corner of the card.

2. Glue the decorative wrapping paper into position in the middle of the 5″ square solid piece.

3. Outline the papers with the gold felt pen.

4. Decorate the 4″ strip with the gold felt pen.

5. Take the 4″ strip of paper and fold it back and forth accordion style to create a fan as indicated in steps 5 though 7 of the previous recipe.

6. Use craft glue to attach the fan to the card as indicated in the diagram.

Tissue FANtasy

MATERIALS:

- 9″ × 6″ light-colored blank, folded to create a 4-½″ × 6″ card

- triangular pieces of solid, bright tissue paper decorated with gold poster paint (see Ch. 6, *Stardust* technique)

- narrow piece of curling ribbon the same color as the tissue paper

- 1″ × 2-½″ strip of gold paper

EQUIPMENT:

gold pen
leather hole punch with a small hole size
hammer
glue stick
metal ruler

X-acto knife
clear-drying craft glue

INSTRUCTIONS:

1. Flatten the card and glue triangular pieces of tissue paper in a pleasing pattern.

2. Outline the paper with the gold felt pen.

3. Take the 1″ × 2-½″ strip of paper and fold it into a fan as indicated in steps 5 through 7 of *FANtasy*.

4. Glue the fan onto the prepared card.

VARIATIONS:

1. The fan itself can be modified by changing its size (and therefore its prominence) or by making it out of a decorative paper. You can also decorate the paper by adding bands of paper in complementary colors.

Kimono

The variations on cards with the kimono fold are endless. I like to make my kimonos out of plain paper and then use ornate paper as a backdrop. This way, the pattern on the fancy paper shows up quite clearly. I think that you will find the kimono easier to fold than the crane.

Kimono instructions

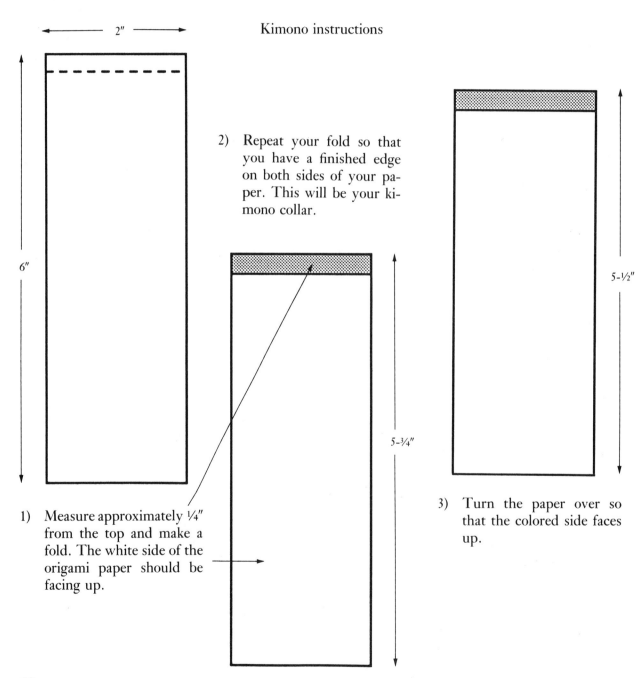

2) Repeat your fold so that you have a finished edge on both sides of your paper. This will be your kimono collar.

1) Measure approximately ¼" from the top and make a fold. The white side of the origami paper should be facing up.

3) Turn the paper over so that the colored side faces up.

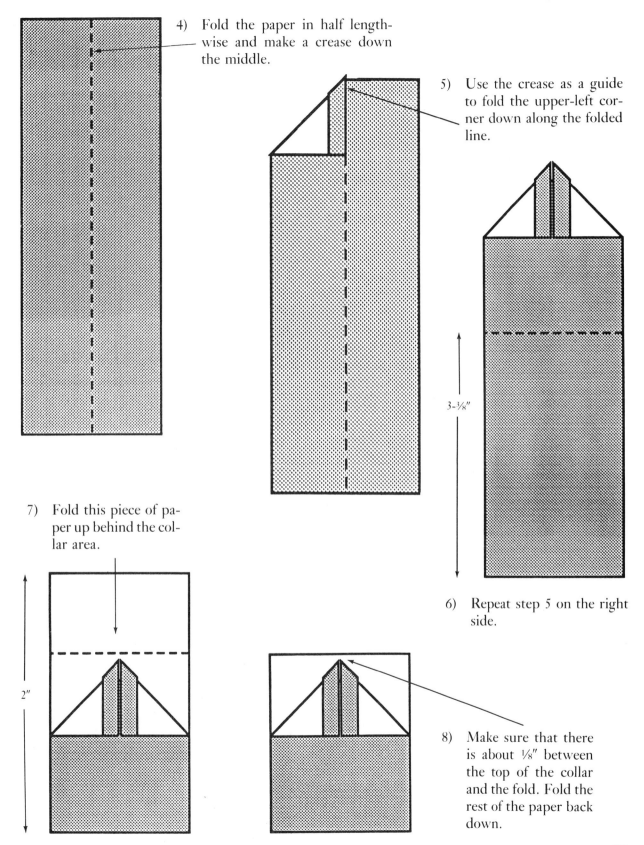

4) Fold the paper in half lengthwise and make a crease down
the middle.

5) Use the crease as a guide
to fold the upper-left corner down along the folded
line.

3-3/8"

7) Fold this piece of pa-
per up behind the col-
lar area.

2"

6) Repeat step 5 on the right
side.

8) Make sure that there
is about 1/8" between
the top of the collar
and the fold. Fold the
rest of the paper back
down.

9) Your model should now look like this. If you look at the profile, you should see an accordion fold.

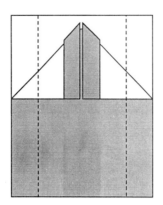

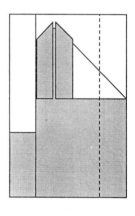

10) Fold both of the outside edges inward to meet the sides of the collar.

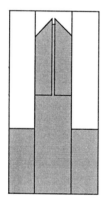

11) Slip your fingers under the first layer of the flaps until it looks like your finger has a hood on it. Then flatten the hood so that the central creases line up.

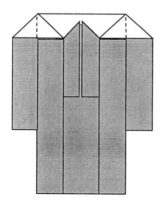

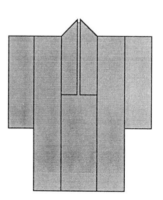

12) Fold back the white area of the kimono so that it is hidden behind the model and glue it down.

Kimono Creation

There are so many wonderful possible combinations with this design. Just remember, the choice of paper will have a strong influence on the outcome of the card!

MATERIALS:

- 6″ × 9″ card blank, folded to create a 4-½″ × 6″ card blank
- 2″ × 6″ piece of plain origami paper or heavy tissue paper
- 2-¼″ square piece of gold paper
- piece of wrapping paper or fancy paper, slightly larger than 4-½″ × 6″
- glue stick

EQUIPMENT:

metal ruler
X-acto knife
ball-point burnishing tool
pencil

INSTRUCTIONS:

1. Apply glue to the back of your fancy paper and press the front of your card down onto it so that the ornate paper completely covers the front of the card. Use your ruler and X-acto knife to trim off the excess paper that extends past the edges of the card.

2. Glue the gold square (turned on its side so it is diamond shaped) on the right-hand side of the card.

3. Fold the 2″ × 6″ paper into a kimono according to the instructions.

4. Glue the kimono onto the gold diamond with craft glue.

VARIATIONS:

1. Take a gold pen and add simple decorations to the kimono. Or, on a plain background, strategically arrange a strip of fancy paper, a piece of solid-colored paper, and the kimono. Pick up one of the colors from the ornate paper with solid-colored dots scattered across your composition.

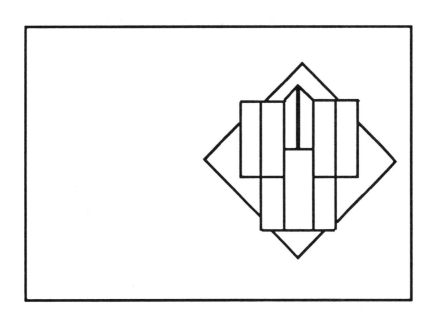

Peace Crane

The most famous origami figure is that of the crane, which has been adopted by the antinuclear movement. In Japanese folklore, the crane represents good health and a life of one thousand years. This is a wonderful image and sentiment to attach to any homemade card.

The crane is a very traditional fold and is always made with a square of paper.

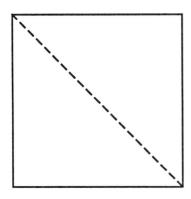

1) Bring upper right corner down to meet lower left.

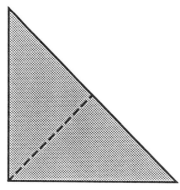

2) Fold in half again, making the lower right meet the upper left.

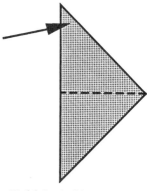

3) Fold in half again, make a crease, and reopen fold.

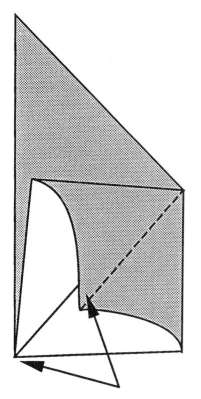

4) Lift corner and open up top layer.

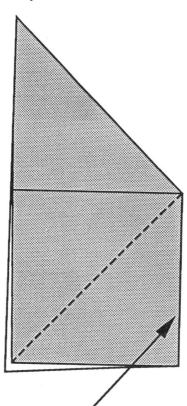

5) Bring the top corner down to meet the bottom, creating a square.

6) Flatten along these two lines.

56

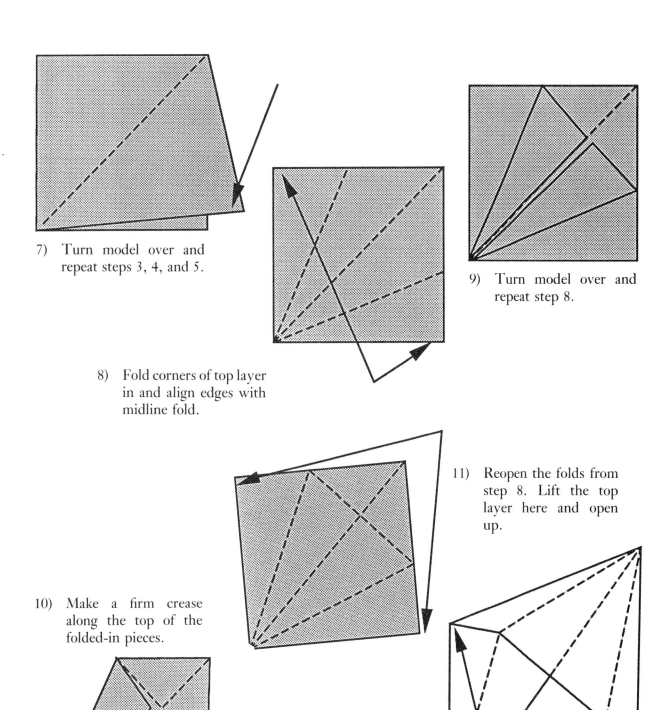

7) Turn model over and repeat steps 3, 4, and 5.

8) Fold corners of top layer in and align edges with midline fold.

9) Turn model over and repeat step 8.

10) Make a firm crease along the top of the folded-in pieces.

11) Reopen the folds from step 8. Lift the top layer here and open up.

12) Fold the two side corners under the top layer so that they align with the crease you made in step 9.

57

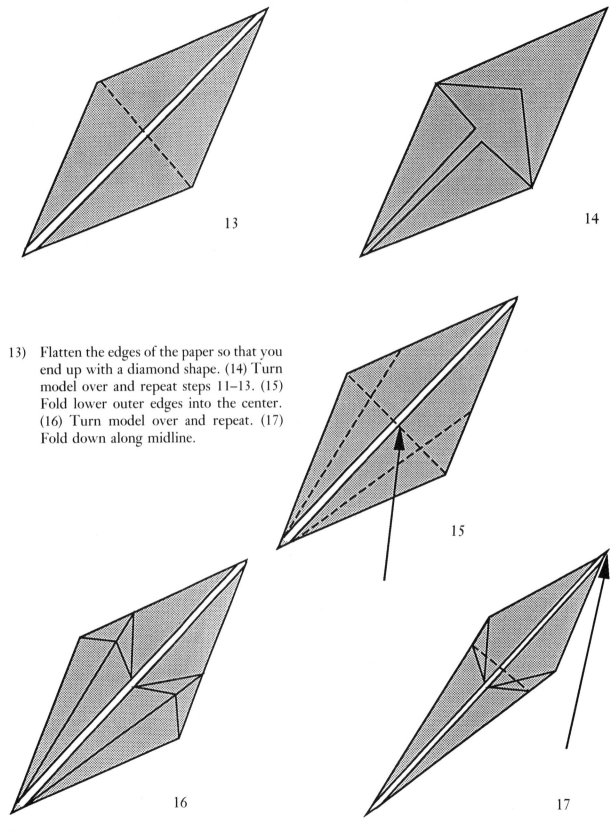

13) Flatten the edges of the paper so that you end up with a diamond shape. (14) Turn model over and repeat steps 11–13. (15) Fold lower outer edges into the center. (16) Turn model over and repeat. (17) Fold down along midline.

13

14

15

16

17

18) Turn model over and repeat step 17. (19) Fold top layer to the left, as if you were turning the pages in a book. (20) Fold point up as far as it will go.

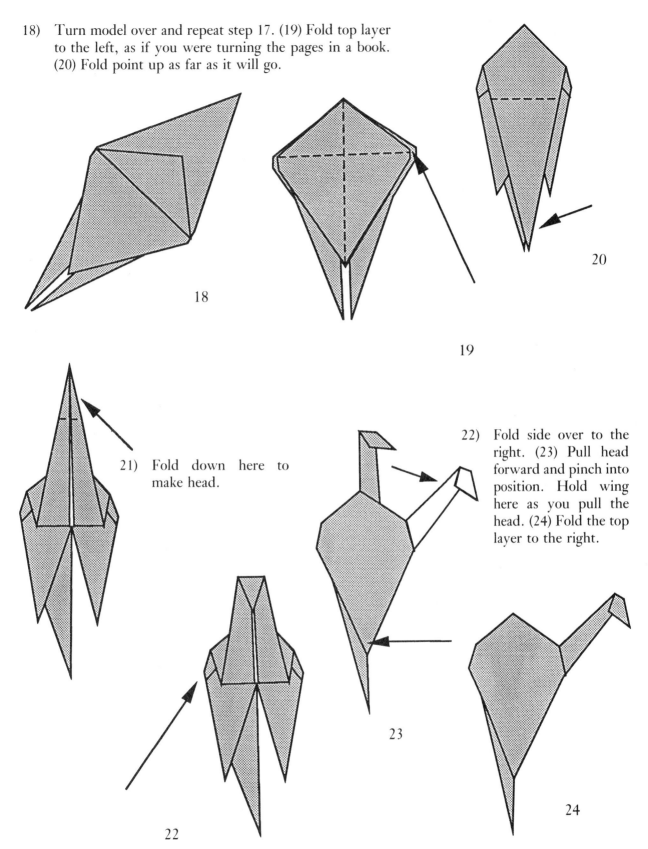

18

19

20

21) Fold down here to make head.

22) Fold side over to the right. (23) Pull head forward and pinch into position. Hold wing here as you pull the head. (24) Fold the top layer to the right.

22

23

24

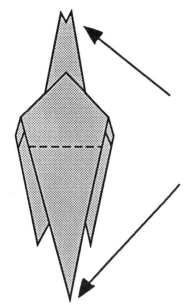

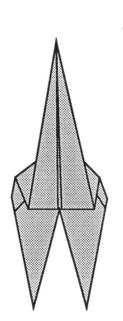

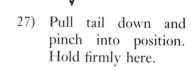

25) Fold the point up as far as it will go.

26) Fold top layer to the left.

27) Pull tail down and pinch into position. Hold firmly here.

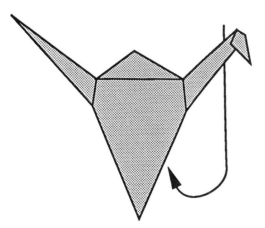

28) Lift back wing to flatten for card.

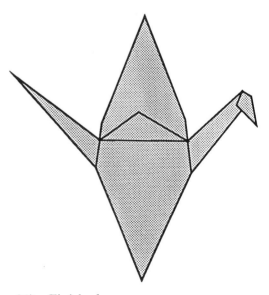

29) Finished crane.

VARIATIONS:

1. When considering the placement of your crane, remember that we read and view compositions from left to right. If you have the crane's head pointed to the right side of the card, it will appear to be moving forward. If the head is facing right and is above the tail, the bird will appear to be flying upward.

2. Because the peace crane is the focal point for any card on which it sits, you do not have to do much more to the card than show off the crane. Some of my favorite variations are to place a solid-colored crane on a square of decorative paper that has been turned on its side like a diamond and add three dots made of the same decorative paper; place a crane on a background of woven paper (see Ch. 4, *Tissue Weave*); place two tiny cranes against a coffee filter background (see Ch. 6, *Soak It Up* technique).

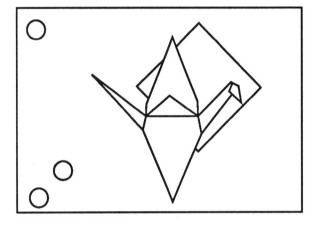

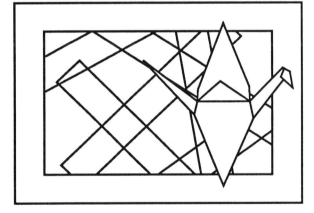

VARIATIONS OF *PEACE CRANE* CARD

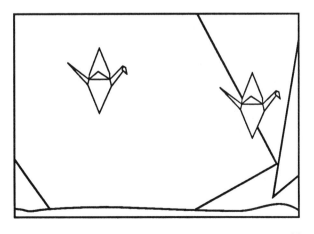

6

Decorating Paper

Throughout this book I have suggested uses for beautiful papers. These materials are a joy to work with and enhance the looks of the cards. However, some of them may not be available to you locally (see Chapter 2, "Purchasing Papers and Supplies"), or may be prohibitively expensive. In any case, you will probably get a lot of enjoyment out of decorating and using your own papers.

This chapter deals with a wide variety of easy and inexpensive techniques for decorating paper and turning it into something that is entirely unique. When completed, the papers can be shown off on their own or used as part of a collage or in conjunction with origami models. It is generally a good idea to decorate a piece of paper and then add it to your card rather than to decorate the card stock itself. In this way, you can experiment with the technique you are trying and only add it to the card if you are truly pleased with the outcome.

As in previous chapters, I will explain how to execute a particular technique, give specific card making examples, and then follow the examples with suggested variations. I hope that this will give you enough information to learn the techniques and will encourage you to experiment creatively with your results!

Bubble Technique

In workshops, people either squeal with delight or squirm in discomfort when I introduce this technique. You will have to decide for yourself which group you belong to.

MATERIALS:

• plain, reasonably absorbent paper

• water

• liquid dishwashing detergent

• water-soluble paint (acrylic or tempera)

EQUIPMENT:

plastic straws
cups
small plates

INSTRUCTIONS:

1. In the cups, mix water, paint, and detergent in equal parts.

2. Place the cup on a plate to catch any overflow.

3. Blow air through the straw until bubbles extend up past the lip of the cup. Remove the straw.

4. Take your paper and, being careful not to touch the rim of the cup, allow the paper to come into contact with the bubbles.

5. Wait for the bubbles that you have caught to pop and—Voila!—bubble paper.

HINTS:

- If your mixture bubbles but will not bubble up past the brim of the cup, you need more water.
- If your mixture does not want to bubble at all, you should add more detergent.
- If the bubbles on your paper are too faint, you need more pigment and should add more paint.

Bubble Card

MATERIALS:

- 5″ × 5″ piece of light-colored paper
- 8″ × 6″ dark-colored card stock, folded to make a 4″ × 6″ card

EQUIPMENT:

metal ruler
X-acto knife
glue stick
bubble-making supplies

INSTRUCTIONS:

1. Decorate the 5″ × 5″ piece of paper using the bubble technique described above.

2. Look at your piece of bubble paper and carefully select what you think is the most interesting portion of it. Cut a 3″ × 5″ section out.

3. Center the 3″ × 5″ bubble paper on the front of your card.

Play until you have a mixture that you are happy with. By adjusting the amount or color of paint you have in your mixture, you can make a multi-layered, decorative bubble paper.

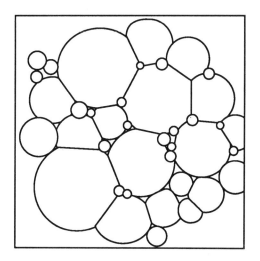

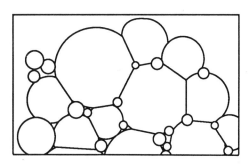

VARIATIONS:

1. If you use quite a bit of paint with a very light pigment and a dark paper, you can get interesting results, for example, white bubbles on black paper. You can create gold or silver bubbles by using a metallic acrylic poster paint. Bubble paper can be used either on its own to show off the technique or as one part in a collage. You can view your bubbles as clouds floating in the sky on a beautiful sunny day and try to "see" something in the images. By adding an eye here or an ear there with a felt pen, you can aid other viewers in "seeing" your hidden image.

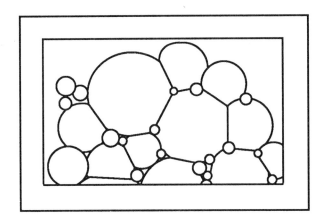

Meltdown Technique

This technique is a fun and inexpensive way of decorating paper to produce richly colored unique designs.

MATERIALS:

- inexpensive white paper (I like to use a 4″ × 6″ piece of rice paper with a bit of a texture to it.)

- a package of wax crayons that includes metallic colors

- aluminum foil

- old newspapers

EQUIPMENT:

a cheap plastic pencil sharpener
an iron

INSTRUCTIONS:

1. Sandwich your white paper between folded layers of aluminum foil and place the whole on a stack of old newspapers.

2. Open the foil so that you expose your sheet of paper. Select the colors you like from the choices provided within the crayon box. Remove the paper covering from the crayons and, using the pencil sharpener, dot the paper with wax crayon shavings. This is an additive process so be careful not to use too much wax at the start.

3. Close the foil sandwich and, with the iron on a medium to hot setting, apply heat for two or three seconds.

4. Open the foil to see what your wax melt looks like. If you are not satisfied, add more wax and try again until you are happy.

5. You can draw on small sections of your paper while it is hot and get the same melted wax look. This is useful if you want to fill in a small area.

VARIATIONS:

1. *Meltdown* paper can be used as a replacement for background decorative paper in almost all projects in this book. By crumbling your foil, you can get a textured look to the melted wax. If you move the iron in one direction with a sweeping motion, it will produce a

At top, a card decorated with an origami fan. Below it, a collage made with decorative paper and gold cord that adorns a textured card base. At bottom, a card with a decorative deckle edge and a triangle composition.

A

This grouping includes two versions of the Back and Forth *motif (top) and a Valentine's Day card that was decorated with a heart pattern made with a cookie cutter.*

B

In the upper portion of the photo at left are two collage cards. In the lower portion is a specially folded announcement card decorated with tissue paper (left) and a design made with a sand-dollar stamp that was embossed with silver thermal embossing powder. Below, clockwise from upper lefthand corner, a diaper-shaped birth announcement, a card with a drypoint-embossed border and monogram, a design made with an angel rubber stamp and a red ribbon, and a card that incorporates rubber stamping, and drypoint and thermal embossing.

C

Three lovely cards that were decorated with collage techniques. At top, Kimono Creation; *at center*, Triangles, Triangles, Triangles; *at bottom*, Floral Meltdown.

D

Upper photo, from left: Half and Half, Aerogram with a Twist, *and* Once Over Twister. *Lower photo:* Dark FANtasy *and* Star Light, Star Bright.

E

At top, clockwise from lower left: Collage with scorpion origami model, Weathergram, collage with origami swan, and woven card. At right, from top: Tissue Weave, Square City, and Interwoven.

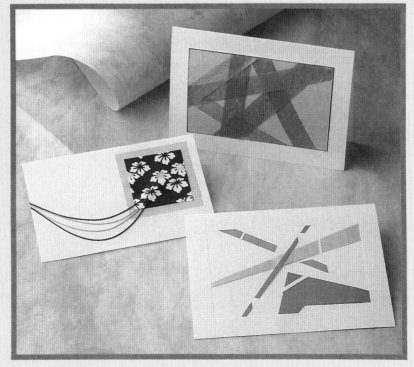

F

Three examples of collage that make use of folded paper creations.

G

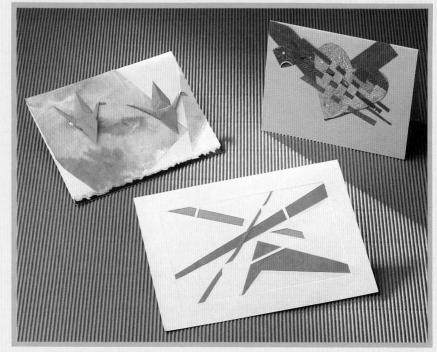

Various styles of interlocking card (above left) and a card that was "stardusted" with gold paint and shaped with a star craft punch (above, right). At right, three examples of cards decorated with collage designs, including an origami creation, a heart with paper strips woven into it, and a cleverly woven set of strips that decorate both the inside and outside of the card.

H

feeling of movement if you have enough wax built up. Add dried flowers to the meltdown with a dot of clear-drying craft glue after the wax has cooled for a very pretty variation. *Meltdown* paper can make a terrific stained glass window in a card or background for an origami model. Try experimenting with different strong-colored cardstock under the *Meltdown* paper, as this can change the feeling of the paper considerably. When using your *Meltdown* paper in making cards, be aware of the fact that the crayon can leave marks on card blanks. This paper does not fold well and will often crack and break if you try to fold it, so this paper must be used flat. The waxy surface is somewhat resistant to glue. It is much easier to get the *Meltdown* to adhere to paper by using a craft glue instead of a glue stick. *Meltdown* papers are often so interesting that they can be used on their own.

Floral Meltdown

MATERIALS:

- 3″ × 3″ piece of rice paper

- a selection of wax crayons in the purple, pink, and silver color range

- 6″ × 9″ piece of gray-flecked card, folded to create a 4-½″ × 6″ card blank

- aluminum foil

- dried flowers (any combination of pink, violet, and white)

EQUIPMENT:

metal ruler
X-acto knife
clear-drying craft glue
pencil sharpener
iron

INSTRUCTIONS:

1. Make *Meltdown* paper according to the instructions above.

2. Glue the *Meltdown* paper onto the card as indicated in the diagram.

3. Place a tiny drop of clear-drying glue onto the back of the dried flowers and add to your card. Place some of the flowers on the wax melt and some on the card paper.

Cookie Card Technique

This is a type of card that anyone from pre-schoolers to seniors can enjoy making. It is not for the perfectionist as you are never sure of exactly what you will end up with. You must use *plastic* cookie cutters to get this to work!

MATERIALS:

- plain piece of paper
- liquid tempera paint in a color that will contrast with your card stock

EQUIPMENT:

plastic cookie cutter(s)
shallow dish for the paint

INSTRUCTIONS:

1. Pour paint into a broad, shallow dish.

2. Dip the cutting edge of the cookie cutter into the paint and use it to print or stamp on your paper.

3. Allow the paint to dry.

Heart Felt

The following recipe makes a very quick but attractive Valentine's Day card.

MATERIALS:

- 5-½″ × 8-½″ light pink card stock, folded to make 4-¼″ × 5-½″ card
- 5″ × 6″ piece of deep pink paper that accepts paint well (e.g., construction paper)
- white liquid tempera paint

EQUIPMENT:

small, heart-shaped plastic cookie cutter
shallow dish for the paint
glue stick
X-acto knife
metal ruler
fine-tipped, black felt pen

INSTRUCTIONS:

1. Dip the cutting edge of the cookie cutter into the paint and use it to print on your deep pink paper. Overlap the hearts and vary the orientation of the cutter. Cover the whole paper.

2. When the paint has dried, cut your deep pink paper to 3″ × 4-¼″ size.

3. Glue the paper to the middle of your card blank.

4. Outline the edge of your paper with the black felt pen.

VARIATIONS:

1. There are a vast number of variations for cookie cards. For example, you can print directly on colored card stock making an overlapping pattern on both the front and the back of the card, print different shapes, or print the same shape but use different colors. You can also combine the printing with collage techniques, print a single shape, three shapes diagonally, or, if you are printing a heart, star, or teddy bear shape and can find sequins of the same shape, add them with craft glue.

Smoke Technique

This is a straightforward technique that gives a wonderful ethereal image. However, this is *not* a procedure to use with children!

MATERIALS:

- piece of light-colored paper

EQUIPMENT:

a sturdy candle

matches

a pail of water (as a safety precaution in case of fire)

INSTRUCTIONS:

1. Light the candle and move the paper through the flame. The paper must actually touch the flame to produce a mark. A sweeping motion gives a nice image. I also like moving the paper up and down over the flame along the same line. Be careful not to touch the candle itself with the paper because you will get a wax mark. If you hold the paper in the flame for too long, you will get a very dark, sooty mark or your paper will catch fire! This technique takes a bit of practice, but it is well worth it.

2. Allow the paper to sit for a moment so that the smoke will set. As an option you can use a fixative on the smoke but I find it unnecessary if the image is light and airy.

3. When you glue the smoke paper to your card blank, place a spare piece of paper over the smoked one when you apply pressure as you press it onto the card. This will insure that you do not smudge the smoke.

VARIATIONS:

1. Use pencil crayons to lightly color some of the smoky areas. This gives the design a wonderful feeling of movement and magic.

Dancing Smoke

This is a good "quickie" card to make if you need one in a hurry and you have already mastered the technique of drawing on paper with smoke.

MATERIALS:

- 5-½″ × 8-½″ dark-colored card stock, folded into a 4-¼″ × 5-½″ card
- 5″ × 6″ piece of light-colored paper that has a dancing smoke drawing

EQUIPMENT:

glue stick

X-acto knife

metal ruler

INSTRUCTIONS:

1. Choose the most interesting portion of your smoke drawing. Cut it down to 3″ × 4-¼″ rectangle.

2. Glue the smoke paper to the center of your card blank.

Stardust Technique

Beware, this technique can be addictive because it is so easily done and gives such a professional finish to your cards.

MATERIALS:

- a jar of acrylic, water-soluble gold or silver poster paint
- water
- good paper
- scrap paper

EQUIPMENT:

cheap sponge
jar lid

INSTRUCTIONS:

1. Mix the concentrated paint with a little bit of water in the jar lid.

2. Tear two pieces from the cheap sponge. Try to make your tears as jagged as possible.

3. Dip one of your sponge pieces into the metallic paint. Use it to lightly add paint to the jagged portions of the other sponge piece. (The sponge that goes directly into the paint usually gets too much paint on it and would give splotches instead of stardust sprinkles if it were to be used directly on the good paper.) Take the second sponge piece and dab it onto your good paper. Use the scrap paper under the good paper so that you can dab the sponge right to the edges and beyond without worrying about "stardusting" your table.

VARIATIONS:

1. Try giving your sponge a little twist as you place it on the paper, vary the amount of paint put on the sponge, or use the sponge to create sweeping lines. This technique works well with all the *Interlocking Magic* cards found in Chapter 3 and Chapter 8. It also works to decorate paper used for making collages such as the *Twister* series from Chapter 4 or *Tissue FANtasy* from Chapter 5.

Star Light, Star Bright

MATERIALS:

- gold acrylic paint
- 6″ × 8″ dark blue paper
- 7″ × 9″ white paper
- water

EQUIPMENT:

metal ruler
cutting board
glue stick
pencil
X-acto knife
jar lid
cheap sponge

INSTRUCTIONS:

1. Fold the dark blue paper in half to form a 4″ × 6″ card.

2. Fold the white paper in half to form a 7″ × 4-½″ card.

3. Put a small bit of glue on the spine of the white card and insert it into the interior of the blue card. Tack the corners of the blue card to the white card while they are both still folded.

4. Trim the white card so that it is the same size as the blue card. This should be done while they are both folded. If you follow these directions carefully you should have a card with a dark blue exterior and a white interior that sits flat and will not buckle.

5. Use the stardust technique to add fine gold dots all over the exterior of the navy blue card.

6. Open the card flat and use your X-acto knife to cut a good-sized star window into the upper-right-hand portion of the card front. When you close the card you will have a white star (the interior of the card) floating in a universe of gold flecks!

VARIATIONS:

1. The whole procedure would be simplified if you could find paper that was navy blue on one side and white on the other. You can use a star-shaped hole punch to make many tiny star windows or you can make the whole card in the shape of a star.

Soak It Up

This is a lot of fun to do with young children and it gives you a chance to play at blending colors.

MATERIALS:

• food coloring

• water

• *very* absorbent paper (coffee filters are best, but you can also use paper towels)

EQUIPMENT:

eyedropper(s)
small containers for water

INSTRUCTIONS:

1. Dilute some food coloring with water.

2. Use the eyedropper to drop some of your colored mixture onto the absorbent paper. Allow the color to bleed.

3. Make your mixture more concentrated or change the color and repeat the procedure until you are happy with your results.

4. Let your paper dry completely before using it.

VARIATIONS:

1. You can presoak your paper and blend wet on wet. Crumple your paper after coloring and allow it to dry with a wrinkled look.

Explore the subtle colors you can make by mixing the primary colors before putting them into your eyedropper. Experiment using water colors instead of food coloring. Add some metallic paint with the *Stardust* method after your paper is dry.

7
Rubber Stamps & Embossing

Rubber stamps and embossing techniques can be used for making multiple cards that have the same design. This chapter will explore some of the different ways of using these decorating methods to make greeting cards.

Rubber Stamps

The joy of working with rubber stamps is that you can consistently repeat the same image over and over with minimal effort. Almost any image imaginable can be made into a rubber stamp, thus allowing a great deal of flexibility.

Rubber stamps may be purchased commercially with a predetermined image, or they can be made in any image that you dream up. If you want to have a custom stamp made (with anything other than words on it), you provide the manufacturer with "camera ready" artwork. Camera ready means solid black on white paper. You can draw, write, print, or photograph your image. However, if you use a photograph, you will have to have it "screened" by a reproduction shop. In this process, they will turn it into a pattern of solid white or black dots just like pictures you see in newspapers. If you decide on words only for your stamp (your name for example), you can usually select from a variety of typefaces and sizes available at the

stamp shop. To find a shop that can custom make a stamp for you, just check under rubber stamps in the yellow pages of your telephone book.

Commercially made stamps are fairly easy to obtain. Most large stationery and educational supply stores carry a variety of them. There are also numerous mail order companies that specialize in rubber stamps. You can buy sets that will allow you to create your own combinations of images, such as alphabets and stamps of different eyes, noses, and mouths. Stamps are great items to look for if you are travelling abroad. Often the images you find will have a local or ethnic flavor to them and are light and easy to carry.

Be selective when you buy stamps. An elegant and beautiful image will lend itself to making an elegant and beautiful card.

My personal preference when buying stamps is to pick either fanciful images, such as a young boy swinging from the moon, or images from nature, such as a sand dollar, a long-stemmed iris, or a burst of stars.

If you are making a lot of greeting cards, particularly if you are selling handmade greeting cards of your own unique design, you should consider having a custom stamp made up that you can use to identify yourself on the back of your cards. I generally stamp either my name or a simple logo.

If you feel particularly industrious, you can

71

make your own stamps by carving pencil erasers.

You will need to get some ink pads to go with your stamps. These come in a wide variety of colors, including such newer variations as neon shades, gold, and silver. There are also rainbow pads that contain more than one hue so that you can blend a number of colors together. Ink pads should be stored upside down so that when you use them, the ink will be at the surface and not pooled under the pad.

Water-soluble felt pens can also be used to draw directly onto the stamp, and, if an impression is taken immediately, they give a good, strong image.

To insure a good clean image, you must completely clean your rubber stamp after each use. Commercial window cleaning fluid and paper towelling work well for this purpose.

In the following recipes, I have chosen images from my collection. Substitution for an image of your preference can be made in any of the following instructions. You can also combine rubber stamp images with many of the collage techniques discussed in Chapter 4.

Abounding Stamps

This recipe is really a variation of *Rectangles Abound* in Chapter 4. I use two strong geometric shapes—the circle and the square—and I follow the compositional suggestion of using an odd number in my arrangement.

MATERIALS:
- 5-¾″ × 8″ piece of pale blue, pink or lavender card stock, folded to create a 4″ × 5-¾″ card blank
- 1-½″ square piece of light blue paper (origami paper works well)
- 1-½″ square piece of light pink paper
- 1-½″ square piece of lavender paper
- 3-½″ square of silver paper

EQUIPMENT:
pad of silver ink
sand dollar stamp (or your choice of rubber stamp)
metal ruler
pencil

glue stick
compass
scissors

INSTRUCTIONS:
1. Use the compass and scissors to draw and then cut a circle with a 1-½″ radius from the silver paper.

2. Use your stamp and the silver ink to make an impression on each of the 1-½″ squares.

3. Measure 2" in from the upper edge of your card and 2" from the right hand edge of your card and mark a small **X.**

4. Glue the midpoint of the silver circle over the **X.**

5. Paste the 1-½" squares as shown in the diagram with the colors in any position you choose.

VARIATIONS:

1. The variations with rubber stamps are endless. Using small squares and repeating the images can be made in a rainbow of colors.

Overlapping Sand Dollars

This is a fun way of adding a bit of extra interest to cards decorated with stamps.

MATERIALS:

- ⅜" × 6-¼" silver foil
- piece of smooth-surfaced, good-quality white paper 6" × 10"
- water
- piece of scrap paper

EQUIPMENT:

a pad of silver ink

a sand dollar stamp (or your choice of rubber stamp)

metal ruler

pencil

glue stick

eyedropper

scissors

INSTRUCTIONS:

1. Measure to the 9-½" mark on both sides of your paper and make a crease. Use the eyedropper method explained on page 14 to create a deckle edge along one of the 6" edges.

2. Carefully fold your paper so that you have about ⅛" border showing below your deckle edge. Your card will be approximately 4-½" by 6".

3. Create a silver border by gluing the ⅜" × 6-¼" silver foil to the bottom inside edge

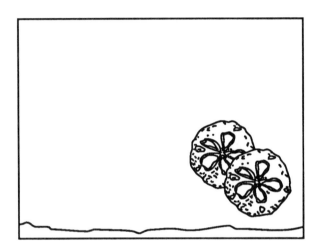

of your card so that it shows below the deckle edge. After you glue the silver paper down, trim the excess length.

4. Stamp a silver sand dollar in the lower right corner of your card.

5. Stamp another silver sand dollar onto your scrap piece of paper. Use your scissors to precisely cut out the image you just stamped. This cut-out piece is called a mask.

6. When the ink on your card is dry, carefully position the mask exactly over the image on the card. Stamp another silver sand dollar, allowing the lower right half of the newest image to be on the mask.

VARIATIONS:

1. Use the mask technique to give your cards a three-dimensional effect or to create interesting borders.

73

Embossing

Embossing means changing the surface level of the card. You can either add something to the card surface to raise it using thermal embossing, or raise or lower the card surface itself by dry-point pressure embossing.

Thermal embossing is traditionally used by printers for wedding invitations, giving the lettering a raised, glossy appearance. To combine thermal embossing with rubber stamps, you stamp your paper and sprinkle embossing powder over the image before the ink is dry. You then heat the image, which causes the thermal powder to bake onto the paper.

Drypoint embossing is done by forcefully moving the surface of the paper up or down with the aid of a stencil and a blunt-ended instrument such as a ballpoint burnishing tool. This is a very simple but elegant technique.

THERMAL EMBOSSING TECHNIQUE

Embossing powder is a fine, sand-like mixture made up of tiny plastic beads that melt when heated. The powder, which can be purchased in most stationers that sell rubber stamps, will stick to anything wet, such as ink or water and honey. There is also a special pad made specifically for embossing that contains a clear mixture that is a little slower drying than ink.

Obtaining an embossed image with a rubber stamp is fairly straightforward. First, use the stamp with either ink pad or embossing pad and place your image on the paper. Then, sprinkle embossing powder over the picture while it is still moist. Shake the paper gently, making sure that the powder has adhered to the complete image. Shake any excess powder onto a scrap piece of paper and then return it to the container (your thermal powder will last forever if you do this). Use a fine watercolor brush to get rid of any stray particles of powder that you do not want baked on.

Once you are satisfied with your image, you heat the powder until the plastic beads melt. It is very obvious when this happens as the whole texture changes and the image becomes very glossy. You can melt your powder by holding the paper under a broiler, or by placing it momentarily on top of a heat source such as an iron, an old electric frying pan, or a coffee hot plate (the backside of the paper should touch the heat source and the powder should face up, exposed to the air).

Thermal powders come in a wide variety of different colors, including pearl blue, gold, silver, copper, pink, and white. You can also buy clear embossing powder to use with colored inks.

Angelica

MATERIALS:

- 7″ × 8-½″ piece of light gray flecked paper
- 3″ × 8″ piece of red paper
- 4″ length of ¼″-wide red ribbon
- silver embossing powder
- embossing stamp pad

EQUIPMENT:

an angel-motif rubber stamp (or your choice of rubber stamp)

leather hole punch   pencil

metal ruler   hammer

X-acto knife

pinking shears (saw-toothed shears)

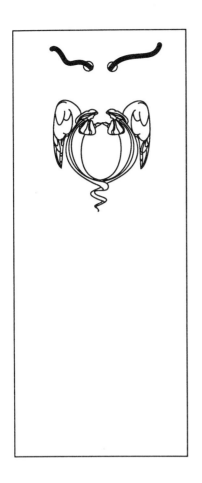

INSTRUCTIONS:

1. Fold the gray paper in half so that you have a 3-½″ × 8-½″ card base.

2. Measure 2-½″ down from the top of the card and equidistant from the edges of the card. Then stamp the angel motif onto the gray card.

3. Sprinkle silver embossing powder over the damp area until your design is very clear. Return the excess powder to the container.

4. Heat the embossing powder until it melts.

5. Use the pinking shears to cut a zigzag edge along both of the 3″ sides of the red paper.

6. Center the red paper in the inside of the card where your message will go.

7. With your leather hole punch and hammer, make two holes fairly close together that are ¾″ down from the top of the card (see diagram).

8. Thread the red ribbon through the holes and tie a simple knot at the front. Trim the ribbon ends at an angle.

VARIATIONS:

1. All the sand dollar recipes can be altered by embossing the patterns. Embossed images may be added to small pieces of paper that are then used in a collage or they can be added directly and very simply to any card stock. You are limited mainly by the design on the stamp itself, so be very selective when purchasing a stamp!

Drypoint Embossing

This technique actually raises or lowers the surface of your design. By using a stencil and a blunt instrument, you can emboss virtually any design on paper.

Drypoint embossing works best on a good-quality paper that has a high "rag" content. "Rag" content refers to the amount of natural fibre, such as cotton or silk, in a piece of paper.

Watercolor papers work well also.

In order to drypoint emboss, you need only a few simple tools. The most important implement is a blunt-pointed burnishing tool of some type, however, you could in desperation use the end of a crochet hook or knitting needle. The best tool that I have found for this job is a ballpoint burnisher. These can be purchased from drafting or graphic stores at a very reasonable price. You also need some way of backlighting your work, that is, shining a light through from underneath. In order of preference, you can use a light table (either a professional graphic artist's one or an improvised one using a glass-topped table), a window during the daytime, or an acrylic recipe holder with a lamp or flashlight shining behind it.

The last piece of equipment you need is a stencil of the form you wish to emboss. This can be made out of thin card or paper. I was amazed to see how insubstantial the weight of the stencil card can be and yet still be effective. You can cut out figures from commercial cards, trace, or draw the design you plan to emboss. Make sure that the silhouette is a strong one and will read well with few details.

DRYPOINT EMBOSSING TECHNIQUE

Place your stencil underneath the paper you want to emboss. Use the backlighting to help you position the stencil. With the aid of your light source, you will be able to see exactly where the shape you are planning to emboss is located.

Either by exercising extreme caution or by using masking tape judiciously, make sure that the stencil is unable to slip away from you as you work on an area. Use your burnishing tool to lightly but firmly trace around the edge of your stencil. That is all there is to it. Take a look at your embossed shape!

It is always best to emboss from the "wrong" side of the paper because sometimes the burnishing makes the paper a little bit glossy. If you want an image that is higher than the rest of the surface on the good side of the paper, you trace around the inside edge of the hole in the stencil. If you desire a shape that is lower on the good side of the paper, you make an island stencil. Do this by gluing the cut out piece onto another sheet of paper and tracing around the outside of the form.

Embossed Card Borders

This is a simple and inexpensive way to make your own embossed-border card blanks. Your success will depend in large measure on the quality of the card stock.

MATERIALS:

- 8-½″ × 11″ piece of lightweight card
- 3″ × 4-¼″ piece of card (cut very carefully with exact right angles)
- craft glue
- pencil
- 5-½″ × 8″ piece of light card stock or good watercolor paper

EQUIPMENT:

metal ruler
ballpoint burnisher
pencil
light table (or other light source)

INSTRUCTIONS:

1. Draw lines on the 8-½″ × 11″ piece of card, as indicated in the diagram.

2. Very carefully, glue the 3″ × 4-¼″ piece of card onto the shaded area (see diagram). Be sure that the glue is entirely dry and the 3″ × 4-¼″ piece of card is fixed firmly to the larger piece before proceeding with step #3. This is your master and can be used repeatedly to make numerous cards.

3. Place the master onto your light table. Then place the 5-½″ × 8″ piece of light card stock or good watercolor paper over the large card so that the corners line up exactly as indicated by the bold angles on the diagram.

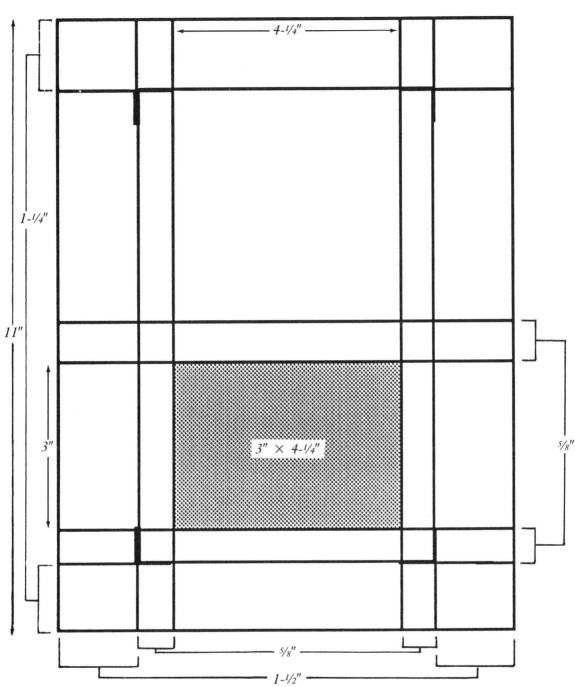

4. Use the ballpoint burnisher to apply pressure to the outside edge of the 3″ × 4-¼″ piece of card that you glued on in step #2.

5. Remove your card and fold it in half so that you have a finished 4-½″ × 5″ card blank with a ⅝″ embossed border.

VARIATIONS:

1. By changing the dimensions on your large sheet of cardboard, you can create numerous masters in different sizes. When creating your masters, remember to take into consideration the available envelope sizes.

Monogram Card

This is a simple yet elegant way of personalizing a card.

MATERIALS:

- 5-½″ × 9″ piece of card stock, folded to create a 4-½″ × 5-½″ card blank

- 3″ square piece of very light cardboard

- tracing paper

EQUIPMENT:

cutting board
X-acto knife
ballpoint burnisher
pencil

INSTRUCTIONS:

1. Choose a letter of the alphabet that you want to use for your monogram. I will use a very stylized **T** as an example.

2. Draw your chosen letter onto a piece of tracing paper. With a pencil, fill in the letter on the tracing paper. Place the paper face down over the lightweight cardboard and use your pencil to apply pressure to the outline of your letter so that the graphite transfers onto the cardboard.

3. Use your X-acto knife to cut out the letter you have drawn on the cardboard to create a stencil and place it on your light table.

4. Use your backlighting to set the open card over the stencil where you want it to appear on the card, making sure that the stencil faces backwards.

5. Take your ballpoint burnisher and trace around the inside edge of the stencil.

VARIATIONS:

1. By finding a book that shows different calligraphic styles, you can vary the letters considerably. You can spell words or combine initials.

Combo Fish

This is a card that combines drypoint embossing, thermal embossing, and stamping. The result is a card with fossil-like images.

MATERIALS:

- clear thermal embossing powder

- bronze or copper thermal embossing powder

- black ink pad

- 2 pieces of 3″ square lightweight cardboard

- 3″ square piece of white bond paper

- 8-½″ × 9″ piece of sandy-colored card stock, folded to create a 4-½″ × 8-½″ card blank

- glue stick

EQUIPMENT:

a rubber stamp of a fish (fairly detailed if possible)
X-acto knife
cutting board
ballpoint burnisher
a jar lid

1. Use the black ink to stamp a fish image onto the middle of the two squares of lightweight card.

2. With your X-acto knife, cut out rough fish shapes, larger than the stamp size, according to the diagrams above. Keep the interior of one of your cutouts.

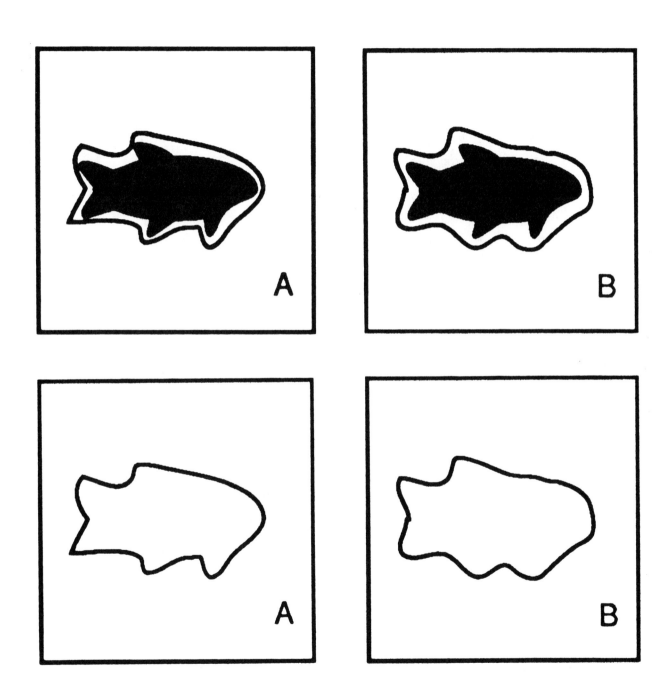

3. Glue the interior of stencil B to the middle of the square of white bond paper. This is an island stencil.

4. In the jar lid, put small amounts of bronze and clear thermal powder. Mix marginally.

5. On your card, stamp three fish images in black, as indicated in the diagram below.

6. Sprinkle the barely mixed thermal powder over the fish images. The rough combination will leave you with some black areas and some bronze areas.

7. Heat fish images to thermally emboss, according to the directions on page 74.

8. Use a light source to place stencil C behind one of your fish images and use your ballpoint burnisher to apply pressure around the outside edges.

9. Place stencils A and B behind the other two fish images and apply pressure around the inside edges. Your finished product will con-

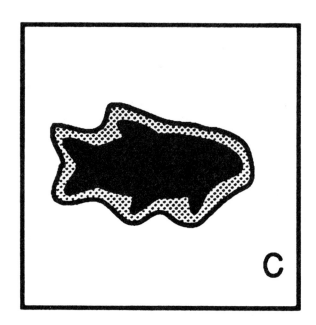

sist of one raised image and two sunken images. I often allow the thermally embossed image to overlap the drypoint embossed images in this application.

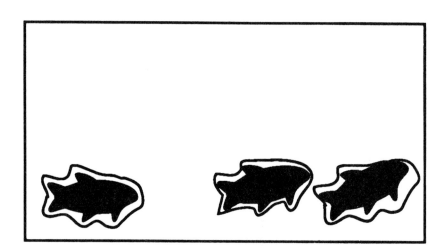

VARIATIONS:

1. Use a mixture of two or three different thermal embossing powders that are roughly blended. This can give you interesting results. By using the island stencil method, you can create a sunken image while still applying the pressure of the burnisher to the back side of the card. Experiment with different ways of combining the two embossing methods!

8
Projects for Special Occasions

It is a special occasion anytime you send or receive a handmade greeting card. There are, however, certain times of the year when we traditionally send greetings to one another and certain life events that are usually marked by the giving of cards. This chapter will address some of the occasions when you are expected to send out cards, such as holidays, "thank-yous," congratulatory events, weddings, and anniversaries, as well as birth announcements and memorial or commemorative cards. The recipes in this chapter are primarily intended to show you how to modify the designs in the earlier chapters of the book to suit a particular occasion.

For invitations and announcements, the information on each card should be the same, although the cards may vary slightly. There are a number of methods available to you if you wish to repeat your message.

Methods for Repeating Information

There are four basic ways to repeat the same message in each card. Any of these methods can be combined with any other one.

HAND WRITE EACH MESSAGE
This is time consuming but gives you a lot of freedom in making subtle little changes from card to card. When choosing to hand write messages, you should consider placement of the text, color, size, and legibility. See A Word on Calligraphy in Chapter 2.

COPY MACHINE
Copy machines are usually readily available (your yellow pages will have a list of copy shops), relatively inexpensive, and fairly easy to prepare a master for. You will get the best results if your master is solid black on white. This can then be copied in black ink onto any color paper you want. The two standard sizes for copying paper are 8-½ × 11 and 11 × 14. If your message is fairly small, you can repeat it a number of times on your master and cut down on your copying costs.

COMMERCIAL PRINTERS
You may decide to have a message commercially printed to insert in your handmade cards. If you choose to go this route, you should work with the print shop from the very beginning. Some printers specialize in small custom jobs and others handle only massive tasks. Look in the telephone book and often the name will give you a clue. Anything with quick, fast, or jiffy in their name is likely to specialize in small jobs. Give them a call and ask before you go to visit them. Remember that you are the consumer and anyone who makes you feel foolish or speaks in technical jibber-jabber is not worth dealing with.

The least expensive way to use a commercial printer is to have everything "camera-ready" when you deliver it. This means that it is exactly the size you want it, exactly as you want it to look, and solid black on white. If you are unable to produce camera-ready work, the printer can usually do the layout work. This means the printer listens to your concept and then does all the preparation for you. However, there is an extra charge for this.

Printers can give you any color(s) you want on almost any type of paper you want. You pay more for each color, and, if you want a specially mixed color, you will get another charge added on. Printers have a paper wholesaler that they buy from, so you can usually choose papers from a sample book.

The best way to deal with a commercial printer is to consult them before you start working on your project. Be sure to check on how much lead time they will need to do your task.

CUSTOM RUBBER STAMP

You can have a rubber stamp custom made to your specifications, usually within a day or two of ordering. (See Chapter 7.) When our second child was born, we had a custom stamp made with all the pertinent information within 24 hours of his birth and at a very reasonable price. I had already made announcement cards complete with slots for a photograph. The stamp made everything so simple that I had all my announcements in the mail before I even left the hospital!

What makes an occasion special varies from person to person and culture to culture. There are numerous books on the market that detail different celebrations marked by various cultures and religions. For example, in France, a person's saint's day (the celebration day of his or her namesake saint) is often considered significant than his or her birthday and in China, there is great importance attached to New Year's celebrations. Some people pay particular attention to the changing of the seasons marked by the solstice and equinox. Each religion has its high and holy days that are impor-

tant to the followers of that faith. The cards in this book can be modified to suit virtually any occasion. The calendar celebrations I have chosen to mention here reflect my own religious and cultural background.

Calendar Celebrations

Color coding is often a good way to indicate a particular holiday. For example, yellow, mauve, and pastels are appropriate for Easter, red and green for Christmas, and fall colors for Thanksgiving.

VALENTINE'S DAY

Valentine's is a celebration that lends itself very well to color coding. Any combination or permutation of red, pink, or white will work well. The heart shape can be used extensively.

The suggestions for creating borders on your cards (see Chapter 3) can be modified to make a decorative lace border. The *Back and Forth* card (page 22) can be done in pink and finished off with a heart-shaped piece of floral wrapping paper attached to the front and outlined in gold. The *Cookie Cutter* technique (page 66) works well with children when making Valentine's cards! Drypoint embossing (page 75) also holds several exciting possibilities.

EASTER

There are many wonderful images associated with spring, flowers, birds, and fresh, bright colors are but a few. The cards decorated with weaving (page 40) can be made with spring colors for wonderful Easter cards. The *Cookie Cutter* technique (page 66), made with bunnies and tulips, gives a strong spring feeling to any card. The peace crane from Chapter 5 is an image of hope and renewal. My favorite Easter cards are those decorated with drypoint embossed (page 75) images of doves and lilies. These are clean, simple, and beautiful.

CHRISTMAS

This is the traditional time of year for sending greetings and keeping up with friends and relations. All the ingredients are in place for a family get-together and festive card-making session.

The red and green color code of Christmas is one way to strongly indicate this festive season without changing the design integrity of your cards. Virtually all the designs in this book can be modified through the use of color to be Christmas cards. The *FANtasy* series works very well when done in red and green.

There are a wide variety of rubber stamps with Christmas images. Any of the card sugges-tions in Chapter 7 work well in a Christmas context. The *Stardust* technique (page 68), in conjunction with stamping and embossing, is very effective for this season.

The use of strong, bold images that are as-sociated with Christmas is another way to in-dicate the season. For instance, the heart shape is used throughout Scandinavia in this festive season and the evergreen tree and star are two common North American images. The follow-ing are modifications of *Interlocking Magic* from Chapter 3.

Interlocking Christmas Magic

MATERIALS:

- 2 strips of paper 3″ × 10″, glued to each other back to back so that they form one strip (The easiest way to do this is to glue two larger sheets together and then cut them down to the 3″ × 10″ format. The paper for the inte-rior must be plain and light in color but the exterior paper could be gift wrap or star-dusted (see page 68) blue or green paper)

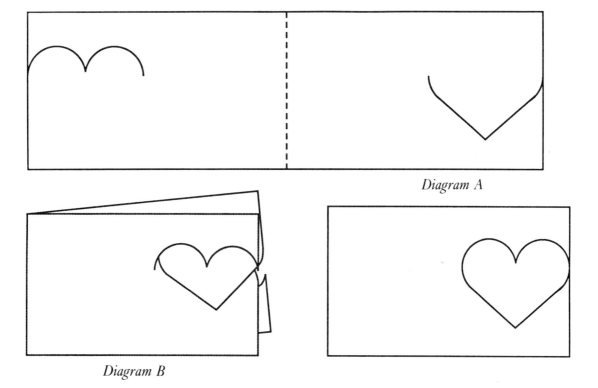

Diagram A

Diagram B

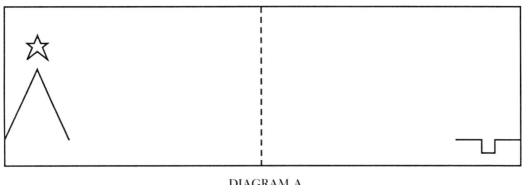

DIAGRAM A

EQUIPMENT:

X-acto knife
pencil
ruler
cutting board

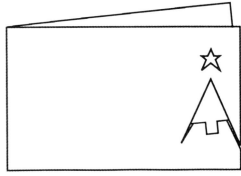

DIAGRAM B

INSTRUCTIONS:

1. Cut your paper as indicated in Diagram A above. You can play with the exact dimensions until you are happy with your proportions.

2. Refold the card interlocking as shown in Diagram B.

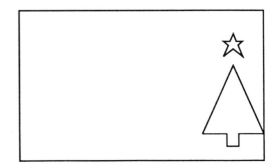

"Congratulations" and "Thank-you" Cards

The *Weathergram* (page 24) is very useful for a quickie thank-you when you do not want to write an extensive message. You can develop a beautiful image on one side and write a line or two on the back. The *Kimono creation* or *Aerogram* will work well for more lengthy thank-you notes.

The exuberant feeling that can be portrayed with the *Twister* (page 34) works wonderfully when sending out congratulatory cards. The *Meltdown* (page 64) technique, especially when it is combined with dried flowers, is another good design when making a laudatory greeting card.

84

Congratulations Card

This is a simple and useful card to have in your basket of ready-to-send cards.

MATERIALS:

- 4″ × 11″ piece of light pink card stock, folded to create a 4″ × 5-½″ card

- 3-¾″ × 13-½″ piece of decorative paper with torn or deckle edges on all four sides

EQUIPMENT:

Calligraphy pens or a rubber stamp that says "Congratulations"

ink pad

metal ruler

pencil

glue stick

INSTRUCTIONS:

1. Measure 1″ in from the bottom of the card and glue down the 3-¾″ side of the 13-½″ strip of decorative paper parallel to the 4″ side of the card. Make sure the remainder of the 13-½″ piece extends past the top of your card.

13-½″

5-½″

Congratulations

Folded Card

2. In the 1″ margin on the bottom of the card, stamp or write "Congratulations." If you use a rubber stamp, you may want to consider using clear embossing powder to thermally emboss it.

3. Wrap the long piece of paper around the back of the card and then fold the last portion to the front so that it overlaps the starting point and covers the message.

This means you have to open two flaps to get to the inside of the card.

VARIATIONS:

1. This design can be used for any occasion, from birthdays to Christmas.

Commemorative and Memorial Cards

When making a memorial card to send to a grieving family or friend, I try to use one of the simple yet elegant collage designs such as *Triangles, Triangles, Triangles* (page 36) or *Rectangles Abound* (page 37). I concentrate on choosing colors and papers that remind me of the person who passed away.

A commemorative card is usually part of a series designed to celebrate the life and personality of the person who died. If the person was close to you, a number of very similar commemorative cards to share with family and friends can be a labor of love. Accordion cards (page 23) work well for this purpose. You can choose a poem, a quote, some photographs, or a series of reminiscences to fill the card's pages.

Commemorative Accordion

MATERIALS:
- 5″ × 18″ sheet of plain, lightweight paper
- 2 sheets of colored card 4″ × 6″
- 2 strands of ribbon, each approximately 12″ long

EQUIPMENT:
metal ruler
pencil
craft glue

INSTRUCTIONS:

1. Fold the 5″ × 18″ piece of paper back and forth accordion style until you have 6 panels that are 3″ wide and 5″ deep.

2. Glue a ribbon to the middle of each side of each colored card. Allow the craft glue to dry completely.

3. Glue a card to one end of the accordion fold paper and make sure that the ribbon pieces are on the inside.

4. Glue the second piece of colored card to the other end of the accordion paper (again with the ribbon on the inside).

5. Tie the ribbons together with bows.

VARIATIONS:

1. You can cover the colored card pieces with a decorative paper, or add a collage (see Chapter 4) to them.

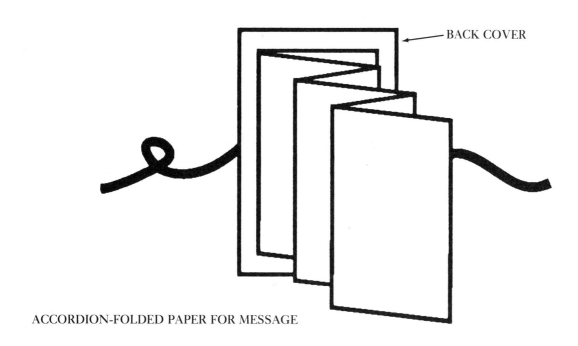

BACK COVER

ACCORDION-FOLDED PAPER FOR MESSAGE

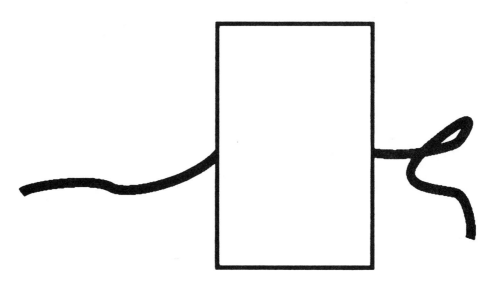

FRONT COVER

Weddings

A commercial printer or calligraphic scribe is probably the best source to use for having your wedding message duplicated many times over. However, there are many great additions that can be made to the printed product. The *Classic Knot* (page 32) and the woven series (pages 41–43) are obvious and appropriate wedding images. Most of the basic collage designs from Chapter 4 work well in a wedding context. For my own wedding, I used the drypoint embossing technique (Chapter 7) to add irises to the invitations.

Baby Announcements

Baby announcements are simultaneously fun and tricky to do. Of necessity, you have to wait until the last moment to get all the information needed for the card. I have developed a couple of different designs that will allow you to complete part of the announcement before the baby's arrival and expediently finish the card after the child is born.

Diaper Delight

This is a simple yet fun announcement belonging to the unique fold category.

MATERIALS:

- 6″ × 11″ piece of paper
- pencil
- diaper pins (one for each announcement)

EQUIPMENT:

cutting board
ruler
hole punch
X-acto knife

INSTRUCTIONS:

1. Cut a triangle out of your piece of paper according to Diagram A.

2. Make a fold line 3-½″ in from both corners on the 11″ side and 4″ from the same corners on the shorter sides (Diagram B).

3. Use your hole punch to make small holes ½″ and 1″ in from the corners, making sure that the holes line up on either side.

4. Make another fold at the 3-½″ mark on the short sides (Diagram C).

5. Fold the diaper and pin with the appropriate color.

VARIATIONS:

1. You can make up all the "diapers" before baby arrives and then hand write or stamp the information on the inside or you could wait until the big day and have the information either copied or printed on colored paper. However, the latter option leaves you with a lot of cutting, folding, and hole punching at the last moment.

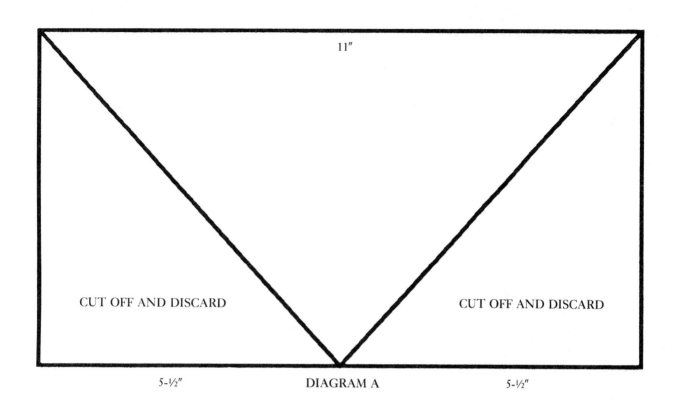

11″

CUT OFF AND DISCARD CUT OFF AND DISCARD

5-½″ DIAGRAM A 5-½″

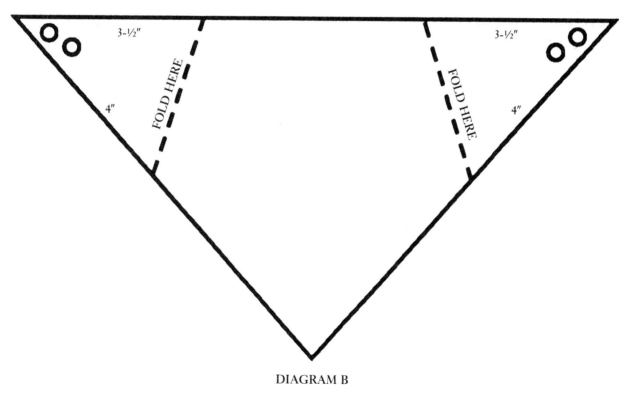

3-½″ 3-½″

FOLD HERE FOLD HERE

4″ 4″

DIAGRAM B

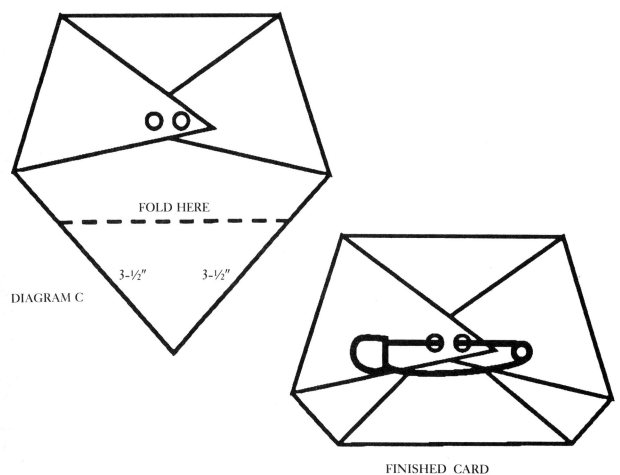

FOLD HERE

3-½"   3-½"

DIAGRAM C

FINISHED CARD

Calling Card

This is a very elegant announcement. All of baby's information is put on the calling card and the rest of the family is recognized on the larger card.

MATERIALS:

- 4″ × 6″ piece of heavyweight, high-quality white paper

- 2″ × 3-½″ piece of the same heavyweight, high-quality white paper

- ¼″-wide velvet ribbon

EQUIPMENT:

cutting board
hammer
ruler
leather hole punch

INSTRUCTIONS:

1. Place the smaller "calling card" on top of the larger sheet of paper in the middle and ¾″ from the top edge.

2. Use your hammer and leather hole punch to make two small holes through both pieces of paper.

3. Pull the velvet ribbon through the holes to tie the two cards together.

VARIATIONS:

1. All of the family information can be put on the card well ahead of time. The ribbon can either be color-coded pink or blue or be prepared ahead of time in a neutral color. Once again, you have your choice of hand writing, printing, or stamping the information.

Susan Jean Pearce
July 17, 1991
8 lbs. 3 oz.

Bill and Diane announce with pleasure their new little bundle of joy !!

Tissue Wrap

The tissue paper used in this design creates a soft, gentle, babylike feel to the announcement. By using mauve, which sits between pink and light blue on the color wheel, you can premake the tissue paper component of the card.

MATERIALS:

- 7-½″ × 9″ piece of light pink tissue paper
- 6-½″ × 8″ piece of light mauve tissue paper
- 5-½″ × 7″ piece of deep mauve tissue paper
- either blue or pink 8-½″ × 11″ copying paper
- pencil
- black felt pen

EQUIPMENT:

cutting board
ruler
scissors

glue stick
office copier machine

INSTRUCTIONS:

1. Center the light mauve tissue paper on top of the light pink piece and tack it in place with one dab of glue. Next, center the deep mauve paper on top of the light pink piece. Make sure you have a light touch with the glue!

2. When the baby arrives, write all the information in black on an 8-½″ × 11″ sheet of paper. This is your master.

3. Have your master copied as many times as necessary onto either pink or blue paper.

4. Center the tissue papers on the back of the copied announcement and make a three-way business-letter fold. Pop the announcement into a business-size envelope and you are done!

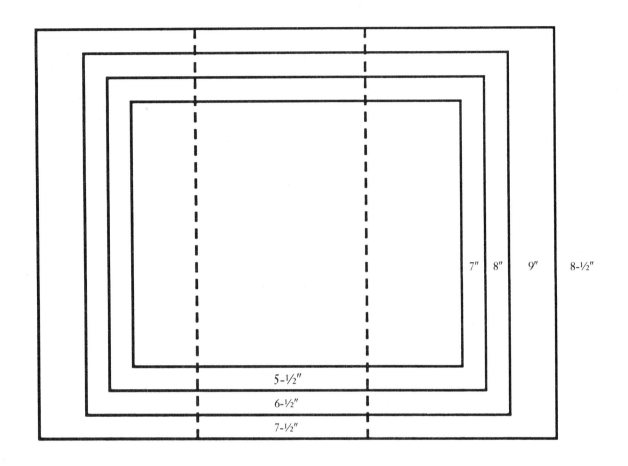

7″ 8″ 9″   8-½″

5-½″

6-½″

7-½″

TURN 90° AND FOLD

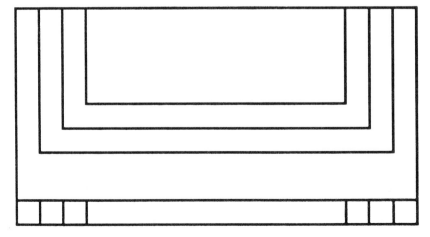

FOLDED CARD

One of the greatest pleasures in making your own greeting cards is to share them with family and friends! Special occasions are the perfect forum for handmade cards. Having a box of card blanks or partially completed cards can be a wonderful way of reducing some of the last minute stress of needing a card for a particular person or occasion. The most important thing to remember if you are to enjoy these opportunities is to *give yourself a comfortable lead time* in order to complete your project. Happy card making!

Glossary

aerogram Lightweight airmail paper that, when folded, serves as its own envelope.

ballpoint burnishing tool A penlike implement with a blunt, ballpoint end that is used to apply pressure to transfer letters or on paper to create an embossed image.

bleeding A graphic design term that refers to an image that appears to flow out past the boundaries of the design.

bond paper 20 lb. paper most commonly known as typing paper.

calligraphy Handwriting done in a careful and measured way.

camera ready copy A master consisting of solid black images on white paper that is prepared for printing or photographing. It is the exact size and likeness of the material to be printed.

card stock A heavyweight paper appropriate for use in making cards.

chiyogami Origami paper on which one side is patterned and the other side is plain.

collage Papers or other 2-dimensional objects that have been arranged together to create a design.

compass A drafting tool used to draw a perfect circle.

craft glue A white glue that dries clear and flexible.

craft hole punch A single-hole punch made to cut out a specific image, for example a heart, star, duck, apple, tree or bear.

custom rubber stamp Unique rubber stamps professionally made to the customer's specifications.

cutting board A board used to cut upon with an X-acto knife so that you do not scar the surface you are working on.

deckle edges A torn-looking edge traditionally found around the edges of handmade paper.

decorative paper Term used to describe any patterned paper, including wrapping paper and chiyogami, also called "fancy paper."

drypoint embossing A method of raising or lowering a paper's surface by applying pressure with a blunt instrument.

duplex paper Paper that is a different color on each side.

embossing A method of changing the surface level of the paper. This can be done by adding to the surface or by causing an indentation in the surface level.

embossing powder Sandlike plastic beads that are baked onto the surface of paper to create a raised surface.

X-acto knife A craft knife with interchangeable blades used for cutting.

glue stick A container of solid glue in a dispenser that is very similar to a solid deodorant stick. Can be purchased in any craft store.

kami The most common type of origami paper. One side is colored and the other white.

kimono Traditional Japanese robe with wide sleeves.

leather hole punch A single-hole punch standardly used for leather. Similar in looks to a screwdriver. A hammer is used to tap the end and force the circle cut in the paper.

light table A table with a light source underneath a translucent working surface which provides backlighting.

mizuhiki Japanese decorative cord used to wrap presents.

model The term standardly used for a completed origami project.

momi A fairly heavy Japanese paper with a crumpled texture.

off-cuts The extra pieces of paper produced when commercial printers trim the excess from large printing jobs.

origami The traditional Japanese art of paper folding used to produce miniature paper models.

rhombus An oblique square more commonly referred to as a diamond shape.

scoring A method of making an indentation in the paper along the line you intend to fold so that the crease can be made neatly.

scribe A person who practices the art of calligraphy.

thermal embossing The technique of raising the surface level of the paper by melting special powder over an image.

Index